KT-539-676

WORLD WAR II

Nigel Cawthorne

igloo

Contents

igloo

Published in 2009 by
Igloo Books Ltd.
Cottage Farm
Sywell
NN6 OBJ
www.igloo-books.com

Copyright © 2008 Igloo Books Ltd.

All rights reserved. No part of this
publication may be reproduced or transmitted
in any form or by any means, electronic, or
mechanical, including photocopying, recording, or
by any information storage and retrieval system,
without permission in writing from the publisher.
The measurements used are approximate.

10 9 8 7 6 5 4 3 2 1

ISBN 978-1-84817-399-6

Designed by The Bridgewater Book Company

Printed and manufactured in China

League of Nations
established in Geneva

Mussolini seizes
power in Italy

Hitler imprisoned after
failed coup in Munich

US stock market
crashes

| 1920 | 1921 | 1922 | 1923 | 1924 | 1925 | 1926 | 1927 | 1928 | 1929 |

THE ROAD TO WAR

WORLD WAR II WAS THE PIVOTAL EVENT OF THE
TWENTIETH CENTURY. LEAVING OVER 50 MILLION PEOPLE
DEAD, IT WAS THE BIGGEST AND BLOODIEST WAR IN
HISTORY. ON ONE SIDE WERE GERMANY, ITALY, AND JAPAN.
ON THE OTHER WERE GREAT BRITAIN, FRANCE, THE SOVIET
UNION, CHINA, AND THE UNITED STATES. MANY SMALLER
NATIONS WERE ALSO DRAWN INTO THE CONFLICT.

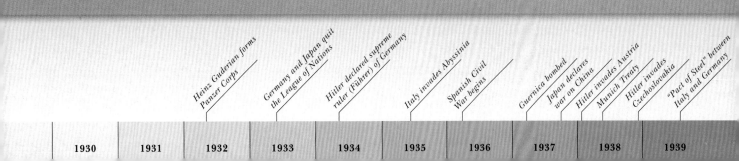

Heinz Guderian forms
Panzer Corps

Germany and Japan quit
the League of Nations

Hitler declared supreme
ruler (Führer) of Germany

Italy invades Abyssinia

Spanish Civil
War begins

Guernica bombed

Japan declares
war on China

Hitler invades Austria

Munich Treaty

Hitler invades
Czechoslovakia

"Pact of Steel" between
Italy and Germany

| 1930 | 1931 | 1932 | 1933 | 1934 | 1935 | 1936 | 1937 | 1938 | 1939 |

The war had its roots in the nineteenth century, when powerful nations had established or consolidated themselves as imperial powers. Even the United States was essentially an empire, having expanded from 13 colonies on the eastern seaboard across the whole of the North American continent and, after 1898, occupying the Philippines. China had been an empire, albeit a decaying one, for millennia and the Soviet Union had expanded eastwards across northern Asia between 1462 and 1894. But Germany and Italy had missed out on the benefits of empire. Formerly loose collections of independent states, they had only unified in centralized nation states in the second half of the nineteenth century. Germany had established some colonies in Africa, but after defeat in World War I—itself an attempt by Germany to expand its presence on the European continent—was stripped of them. Italy had been on the side of the Allies during World War I, fighting against Germany and Austria, and had established a presence in Libya, Somalia, and Abyssinia. But it was eager to expand its African possessions to rival those of Britain and France.

JAPANESE EXPANSION

Japan had also fought on the side of the Allies in World War I. But like Germany and Italy, it had come to the imperial age late. Japan had only been forced to open its ports to international trade in 1853. Its imperial advance was quick,

Mussolini visits Hitler (ABOVE)
Hitler and Mussolini in Munich, Germany, 1940.

European countries (RIGHT)
Map of the boundaries of European countries after World War I.

defeating the Russians in the war of 1904–05, occupying Korea in 1908, and gradually expanding its presence in Manchuria. However, as a victor in World War I, Japan felt it should have been rewarded with more of the postwar German concessions

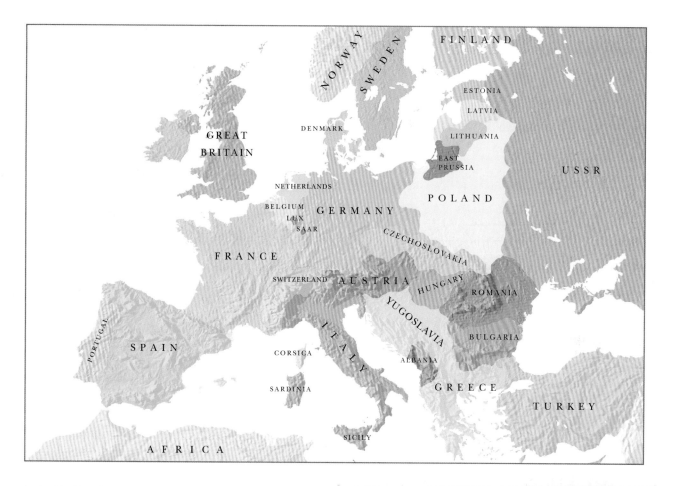

in the Far East. So the battle lines were drawn between aggrieved nations bent on imperial adventures through military means and those nations already enjoying the fruits of empire. Although the ambitions of the belligerent nations were thwarted, World War II eventually resulted in the destruction of the overseas empires of the British, French, and Dutch. The Soviet Union expanded its empire into eastern Europe and north Korea, while the United States increased its influence in Western Europe.

TOTALITARIANISM VERSUS DEMOCRACY

There was also an ideological element to World War II—particularly in Europe and the American war effort in the Far East. The principal Western Allies—Britain, America, Canada, Australia—were liberal democracies. They pitched themselves against authoritarian nations in the name of human freedom. Ironically, these liberal democracies were forced to ally themselves with another authoritarian power, the Soviet Union, which had huge resources, in order to defeat Germany and Japan. After 1945, the Soviet Union capitalized on its part in the victory to strengthen its position with the creation of satellite Communist states in Eastern Europe.

Japan invades China (FAR LEFT)
The aftermath of a Japanese air raid on the Zhabei district, Shanghai, China, 1937.

Peace for our time? (ABOVE)
British Prime Minister Neville Chamberlain emerges from critical meeting in Munich, Germany, 1938.

The Versailles Treaty

"We shall have to fight another war all over again in twenty-five years time at three times the cost."

British Prime Minister David Lloyd George on the Versailles Treaty

The 1914–18 War set the stage for World War II. With the capitulation of the Soviet Union following the Bolshevik Revolution of 1917, Germany felt that its victory was assured. It swung all its forces that had been fighting on the Eastern Front to face the Allies in the West. In the spring of 1918, the Germans broke through and made considerable gains.

Germany's seemingly assured victory was snatched from it by the intervention of the United States, which had joined the war on the Allied side in 1917, and the deployment of large numbers of tanks, developed by the British, which began to prove themselves as war-winning weapons. Meanwhile, starving civilians in blockaded Germany began to revolt. Communists and socialists took to the streets. The Kaiser fled and on November 11, 1918, an armistice was signed in a railway carriage in the forest of Compiègne, the site of the German headquarters in northern France. Though the terms were harsh, this was not an unconditional surrender.

THREAT OF MILITARY OCCUPATION

Details of the peace treaty were to be worked out at a peace conference in the Palace of Versailles outside Paris the following year. In June 1919, the German delegation was forced to sign a peace treaty that had been pushed on them under threat of military occupation. They complained that it violated the Fourteen Points drawn up by US President Woodrow Wilson in October as a basis for peace.

WAR GUILT

Under the treaty, Germany had to admit that it was guilty of starting the war and make reparations amounting to $33 billion, even though economists said that sum could never be paid without disrupting the international financial system. Around ten percent of Germany's territories were ceded to neighboring states. As part of this agreement, Poland was re-established as a country. Germany was also stripped of its colonies. The German Army was restricted to 100,000 men, and Germany was forbidden to manufacture planes, tanks, armored cars, or ships over a specified size. The treaty also provided for the creation of the League of Nations. However, crucially, the US Senate felt the treaty was unfair to Germany and refused to ratify the treaty.

A NATION BETRAYED

"…We came to Versailles in the expectation of receiving a peace proposal based on the agreed principles. We were firmly resolved to do everything in our power with a view of fulfilling the grave obligations which we had undertaken. We hoped for the peace of justice that had been promised to us. We were aghast when we read in documents the demands made upon us, the victorious violence of our enemies. The more deeply we penetrate into the spirit of this treaty, the more convinced we become of the impossibility of carrying it out. The exactions of this treaty are more than the German people can bear …"
Letter from the leader of the German Delegation, Count von Brockdorff-Rantzau, to President Georges Clemenceau, Versailles Peace Conference, May 1919

The Hall of Mirrors (LEFT)
The peace treaty ending World War I was signed in the Hall of Mirrors at the Palace of Versailles, France, June 28, 1919.

The big three (BELOW)
Georges Clemenceau (France), left, Woodrow Wilson (US), center, and David Lloyd George (UK), right, at the Versailles Peace Conference.

The war clouds gather

"By the National Socialist revolution, the German form of life has definitely been settled for the next thousand years."

Adolf Hitler

World War I had widely been regarded as the "war to end all wars"—or that's what people had hoped. But by 1932, the British backbench MP Winston Churchill was warning against German rearmament, though he did not oppose the Japanese expansion into Manchuria, and continued to praise Mussolini up to 1937.

War clouds were gathering. In 1933, both Japan and Germany quit the League of Nations. Hitler was now staging huge rallies in specially-built parade grounds in Nuremberg where, in 1934, he declared a Reich that would last for a thousand years. This was to be the Third Reich. Meanwhile, other totalitarian regimes were gaining ground.

Troops invade (LEFT)
*Italian infantry on the march in
Ethiopia (Abyssinia), 1936.*

have cut Italian supply lines, because Britain still hoped that Italy would be an ally in any forthcoming war with Germany. But Italy, thus condemned over the invasion of Abyssinia, found natural allies in Germany and Japan, who had already pulled out of the League of Nations.

THE SPANISH CIVIL WAR

In July 1936, part of the Spanish Army under Generalissimo Francisco Franco rebelled against the left-wing Republican government, precipitating the Spanish Civil War. Germany and Italy backed Franco. They sent military assistance and used the war to test new weapons and tactics. Although the Spanish terrain was not suitable for massed tank warfare, the German airborne Condor Legion developed the new strategy of "carpet bombing" when they attacked the undefended Basque market town of Guernica on April 26, 1937, killing at least 200 people and wounding many more. By January 1939, Franco had crushed all opposition in Spain.

THE ITALIAN EMPIRE

In October 1935, the Italians began a full-scale invasion of Abyssinia—modern-day Ethiopia. It was an uneven match. The Abyssinian Army were armed with pre-World War I rifles, while the Italians used armored vehicles, airplanes, and mustard gas against them. The Abyssinian Emperor Haile Selassie sought refuge in England. He made a notable speech to the League of Nations, which applied economic sanctions against Italy. However, the British did not close the Suez Canal, which would

SLAUGHTER AT GUERNICA

"As we drew nearer, on both sides of the road, men, women, and children were sitting dazed. I saw a priest in one group. I stopped the car and went up to him. His face was blackened, his clothes in tatters. He couldn't talk. He just pointed to the flame, still about four miles away, then whispered: 'Aviones … bombas … mucho, mucho.' In the city the soldiers were collecting charred bodies. They were sobbing like children. There were flames and smoke and grit, and the smell of burning human flesh was nauseating. Houses were collapsing into the inferno."
Reporter, Guernica, April 27, 1937.

Spanish rebels (LEFT)
*A group of captured Republicans, escorted by Nationalist
troops, Spain, 1936.*

Appeasement

"… a British Prime Minister has returned from Germany bringing peace with honour. I believe it is peace for our time."

Neville Chamberlain outside 10 Downing Street, September 30, 1938

One of Hitler's stated aims was to reunite the German people in one realm or "Reich." In January 1935, a referendum in Saarland, an important industrial area, returned the disputed territory from France to Germany. Then in March 1936, German soldiers goosestepped into the Rhineland in defiance of the Treaty of Versailles. The French were thrown into confusion. The British began to rearm.

Those who thought that Hitler only wanted the return of territories taken from Germany by the Versailles Treaty had to think again. In February 1938, Hitler invited Kurt von Schuschnigg, the chancellor of his home country, Austria, to visit Berchtesgaden in Bavaria. Hitler forced von Schuschnigg to agree to allow members of the Austrian Nazi Party to join his government. The Nazis wanted an *Anschluss,* or "union," between Austria and Germany. Von Schuschnigg announced a vote on the issue of union but was forced to cancel it and resigned. After several unsuccessful political ploys, Germany simply marched into Austria on March 12, 1938. The enthusiastic reception given to the Nazis persuaded Hitler formally to annex his homeland the following day. The result was confirmed by a tightly controlled election where 99.9 percent of voters approved the Anschluss. The vote took place in polling stations full of uniformed Nazis, and voters were given a gilt badge bearing a picture of Hitler's head after they had voted "yes." Within days, the Nazis were boasting that the "great spring-cleaning of Jews" in Austria was underway. The Jewish psychiatrist Sigmund Freud fled to England; the theater producer Max Reinhardt to the US. It was now plain that Hitler would continue making territorial demands. Next he asked for the Sudetenland in western Czechoslovakia, which was heavily populated by German speakers. On April 29, 1938, Britain and France signed an agreement guaranteeing the integrity of Czechoslovakia.

"SELL-OUT TO FASCISM"

Meanwhile, Britain's Conservative Party signed a deal with Mussolini, recognizing his annexation of Abyssinia. In return Italy promised to remove its troops from Spain, where the Civil War was drawing to a close anyway. The opposition British Labour Party condemned the government's pact as a "sell-out to Fascism." Despite these diplomatic maneuvers, the German threat to Czechoslovakia continued. Meanwhile, to the east, Stalin, the leader of the Soviet Union, who had everything to

Chamberlain's paper
British Prime Minister Neville Chamberlain waves his "prelude to peace" at Heston Aerodrome, London, 1939.

fear from Hitler, was less than prepared for war. After purging the Red Army of most of its experienced officers, he was making further purges in the highest ranks of the administration.

APPEASEMENT

While Hitler continued to make territorial demands and sought to overturn the provisions of the Versailles Treaty, the other European nations tried desperately to maintain peace by diplomatic means. This policy, which British Prime Minister Neville Chamberlain proudly called "appeasement," came to be seen as a craven surrender to German demands and helped convince Hitler that the Western democracies were too weak to oppose him.

Some three million people of German origin lived in the Sudeten region of western Czechoslovakia and in May 1938 it became known that Hitler was planning to invade. Britain and France had guaranteed the integrity of Czechoslovakia, which also had a treaty with the Soviet Union. But neither Britain nor France had made the necessary military preparations to defend Czechoslovakia. While Hitler made inflammatory speeches demanding that the Sudeten Germans be reunited with Germany, Chamberlain agreed to fly to Berchtesgaden to talk personally with Hitler who, to Chamberlain's horror, upped his demands, insisting that the Czechoslovak population evacuate the area.

MOBILIZATION

The Czechoslovaks rejected Hitler's demand and mobilized. France followed suit. In a last-minute effort to avoid war, the British, French, Germans, and Italians convened a four-power conference in Munich, the birthplace of Nazism. Mussolini submitted a peace plan, subsequently discovered to have been written by the German Foreign Office. It proposed the German occupation of the Sudetenland, with the fate of other disputed areas to be settled by an international commission. France and Britain acquiesced. Chamberlain returned to England with a piece of paper to this effect, signed by Hitler, and the Czechoslovaks were told they had to submit to the occupation or face the German Army alone. They complied and the Germans occupied the Sudetenland in October and the rest of the country the following March. Hitler then turned his attention to Poland. Britain and France leapt to Poland's defense, signing a military alliance. But the totalitarian states were on the march. In April, Mussolini occupied Albania and, in May, Germany and Italy signed a new political and military alliance known as the "Pact of Steel."

1939–Timeline

Britain & France
mobilize troops

Molotov–Ribbentrop
non-aggression pact

Germany invades
Poland

Operation Pied Piper

Britain and France
declare war on
Germany

France attacks
Germany

Red Army invades
Poland

JULY	JULY	AUGUST	AUGUST	SEPTEMBER	SEPTEMBER

1939

WAR BREAKS OUT

BY 1939, THE WORLD WAS ON THE BRINK OF WAR. FRANCO HAD SWEPT TO POWER IN SPAIN. MUSSOLINI PROCLAIMED HIS NEW ITALIAN EMPIRE. BRITAIN AND FRANCE HAD FAILED TO DEFEND CZECHOSLOVAKIA. HITLER SEEMED UNSTOPPABLE. HE HAD SEIZED POWER FOR HIMSELF AND PERSECUTED COMMUNISTS, HOMOSEXUALS, AND JEWS, WHO WERE STRIPPED OF THEIR RIGHTS AND CITIZENSHIP. MEANWHILE, BRITAIN SCRAMBLED TO REARM AND REINTRODUCED CONSCRIPTION.

"Phony War" starts

Royal Oak sunk by U-boats

Red Army invades Finland

Battle of the River Plate

Admiral Graf Spee scuttled

| OCTOBER | OCTOBER | NOVEMBER | NOVEMBER | DECEMBER | DECEMBER |

Many feared that war would break out over Danzig—modern-day Gdansk. A Polish port, it had been seized by Prussia in 1772 and later absorbed into a united Germany. The Versailles Treaty made it a Free City under the League of Nations mandate, though it lay in the corridor that gave Poland access to the Baltic. The Polish Corridor also split East Prussia off from the rest of Germany. Because Danzig was predominantly German, Hitler demanded its return, giving Germany a corridor to East Prussia. The Poles resisted, so the Nazis began smuggling arms and military advisers into the city. Polish inhabitants were attacked and those who worked in the shipyards were arrested and deported to German concentration camps. Britain and France promised to go to Poland's aid. But after the Allies' abandonment of Czechoslovakia at Munich, this seemed to the Nazis an empty threat. The only nation that could guarantee Poland's security was the Soviet Union, which Britain and France began to woo.

THE MOLOTOV–RIBBENTROP PACT

On August 23, 1939, Soviet leader Joseph Stalin shocked the world by signing a non-aggression pact with Germany. Communists had fought against Franco in Spain and, until this point, the Soviet Union had been seen as the implacable enemy of Nazism—indeed, Hitler was an outspoken anti-Communist. Seemingly out of the blue, German foreign minister Joachim von Ribbentrop flew to Moscow to negotiate the Pact with his Soviet counterpart Vyacheslav Molotov, which promised that their two countries would not go to war with one another. Proposing a toast after the signing ceremony in the Kremlin, Stalin said: "I know how much the German people love their Führer. I should therefore like to drink his health." The Pact included agreement on a secret annex dividing Poland and Eastern Europe. Germany would take western Poland up to Brest-Litovsk. The Soviets would get eastern Poland, Bessarabia (modern-day Moldova and part of the Ukraine), Latvia, Lithuania, Estonia, and Finland.

Awaiting departure (BELOW)
British soldiers wearing carnations prepare to leave for France, 1939.

Breaking the barrier (ABOVE)
German troops destroy a border turnpike between Germany and Poland, 1939.

Nazi-Soviet Pact (RIGHT)
Vyacheslav Molotov and Joachim von Ribbentrop sign a treaty of non-aggression, Moscow, 1939.

MANNING THE BORDERS

By August, the call-up was already under way in Britain, France, and Poland. Switzerland mobilized, and Belgium manned its borders and anti-aircraft defenses. The British Admiralty closed the Baltic and the Mediterranean to merchant shipping. In London, art objects from the British Museum and other galleries were removed for safekeeping. Hitler then sent a message via a Swedish intermediary offering Britain a pact. Germany would respect the integrity of the British Empire if Britain would help Germany secure Danzig and its other territorial demands in Poland, and return the colonies taken from Germany in 1918. Britain declined the offer because it was pledged, with France, to defend Poland if it was attacked. Now nothing could stop the war.

The invasion of Poland

"Usually I awoke to the sound of soft music, but ... martial music blasted into my sleeping area. Then in a few minutes Goebbels ... came on the radio with a special news report announcing that our troops had crossed into Poland."

Herbert Otto Winckelmann, Berlin, September 1, 1939

On the morning of September 1, 1939, a German army of 1.25 million men, including six amored divisions and eight motorised divisions with amored units, crossed the border into Poland behind a heavy aerial bombardment.

Hitler had ranted about Danzig and the Polish Corridor, but the northern wing of his attack headed for Warsaw, while the southern wing swept through Krakow and Lodz.

Leading the attack was Panzer pioneer General Heinz Guderian, who recalled: "On 1 September at 04:45 hours, the whole corps moved simultaneously over the frontier. There was a thick ground mist at first which prevented the air force from giving us any support. I accompanied the Third Panzer Brigade, in the first wave, as far as the area north of Zempelburg where the preliminary fighting took place. Unfortunately the heavy artillery of the Third Panzer Division felt itself compelled to fire into the mist, despite having received precise orders not to do so. The first shell landed 50 yards ahead of my command vehicle, the second 50 yards behind it. I reckoned that the next one was bound to be a direct hit and ordered my driver to turn about and drive off. The unaccustomed noise had made him nervous, however, and he drove straight into a ditch at full speed."

THE POLISH DEFENSES

Although the Polish Army would have outnumbered the attacking German army—the *Wehrmacht*—once it had all been mustered, the Germans were met by 17 ill-equipped infantry divisions. The Poles had just one armored brigade—660 tanks in all, versus Germany's 2,100. The last cavalry charge in history was made by Polish horsemen against German tanks. While the Polish Air Force had just 842 obsolescent planes, the German air force—the *Luftwaffe*—could put 4,700 modern aircraft in the air, trained in the terror tactics used at Guernica. In just seven days, the Panzers reached Warsaw. Although the garrison held out until the 28th, by then much of the city had been reduced to rubble.

On September 17, the Red Army moved across Poland's eastern border to occupy the 76,000 square miles of land, with its population of 12.8 million, promised under the Molotov–Ribbentrop Pact. Condemned internationally, the Soviet Union was expelled from the League of Nations, which had once again proved itself powerless. By the end of September the invasion was complete. The Polish government had fled into Romania. Some 60,000 Poles were dead, 200,000 injured, and 700,000 taken prisoner.

THE GERMAN ARMY ENTERS POLAND

"The bow waves crashed around the tanks, spraying a cool shower over many a driver who crosses the river too fast. To our left is a blown-up railway bridge, at the edge of the road is a dead Polish soldier. It really is a strange feeling to know that now we have left Germany and are standing on Polish soil. Far away we hear the weak barking of a machine gun. Somewhere there is a hollow thunder of cannon—the first signs of war ..."
First Lieutenant W. Reibel, on crossing the Polish border, September 1, 1939

German advance (LEFT)
*German tanks and infantry
advance across the Polish
countryside, 1939.*

Horses in war (BELOW)
*Polish cavalrymen charge across
a field towards German tanks,
September 1939.*

War is declared

"This country is now at war with Germany. We are ready."

Neville Chamberlain, House of Commons,
London, September 3, 1939

After the German army rolled across the Polish border, British and French ambassadors in Berlin delivered identical messages to the German Foreign Ministry. These declared that if Germany did not withdraw her troops, Britain and France would "fulfil their obligations to Poland without hesitation."

Britain had given Germany a deadline for her withdrawal from Poland—09:00 hours on September 3. Two hours after the deadline had passed, Prime Minister Neville Chamberlain declared war. At midday, the French ambassador in Berlin called the German Foreign Minister, Joachim von Ribbentrop, who told him that Germany refused to halt her invasion of Poland. France declared war at 17:00 hours. As it was, there was little Britain and France could do to help Poland. The French Army had been prepared for defense, not attack, and there were no British forces on the Continent until the first part of the British Expeditionary Force took its place in the line at Lille, in France, on October 3. Nevertheless the French did attack Germany on September 7 along the narrow frontier between the Rhine and the Moselle rivers. The Germans held the high ground and salients (outward bulges in a line of fortification) into French territory. They had booby-trapped houses and laid anti-tank and anti-personnel mines in well chosen fields. The French stood no chance. They did not even possess any mine detectors.

THE SIEGFRIED LINE

Beyond the border was the Siegfried Line, a German defensive wall built during the 1930s. To attack it, the French had to bring their own artillery within range of the German batteries, which were well-defended inside concrete casemates. French 155mm shells made little impression and the heavier 220mm and 280mm shells were not fitted with delayed action fuses which would have let them penetrate the casemates before exploding. Although French fire was rapid and accurate, many of their shells, which were of World War I vintage, failed to explode. On September 27, 1939, before the Germans had even taken Warsaw, Hitler told his

Zero hour approaches
Crowds gather at London's Big Ben as Chamberlain's deadline passes, London, 1939.

generals that an offensive should be launched immediately against France. Hitler had wanted to defeat France, particularly, to erase the humiliation of Germany's defeat in World War I. The attack should come as soon as possible because the Western Allies were ill-prepared for war and could only get stronger. Plans were laid to launch an attack between October 20 and 25.

THE PHONY WAR

Britain and France watched the German build-up on the borders of Holland and Belgium with growing disquiet, but heavy rain that autumn meant that Hitler had to postpone the attack no fewer than 13 times. Due to the lack of action, that period became known as the Phony War.

OPERATION PIED PIPER

Bombing had been used during World War I. In Britain, some 564 people were killed and 1,370 injured by Zeppelin attacks between January 1915 and October 1917. Since then, the world had witnessed the carpet bombing of Guernica and European cities had prepared themselves for air attacks. One defensive tactic was the mass evacuation of civilians who did not need to be there.

In the first four days of September 1939, nearly three million people were transported from British towns and cities thought to be in danger from enemy bombers to places of safety in the countryside. This was the largest concentrated

mass movement of people in British history. Most were schoolchildren, who had been labeled like pieces of baggage. Separated from their parents, they were accompanied by an escort of some 100,000 teachers. The order to evacuate was issued at 11:07 hours on August 31, 1939. Within a week, nearly a quarter of the population of Britain had a new address.

STOCKPILED COFFINS

There had been predictions of four million casualties from air raids in London alone. The British government stockpiled coffins and, as a defensive measure, they deployed barrage balloons, whose cables were capable of destroying low-level bombers. Meanwhile, parents were encouraged to send their children to school with a change of clothing, a toothbrush, comb, handkerchief, gas mask, and a bag of food for the day. From the schools, they were bussed to train stations. Arriving in the countryside, they were parceled out by billeting officers to families who were to take them in. Hosts received money for each evacuee they took in but billeting was compulsory, and those who refused to accept evacuees into their homes without a good reason could be taken to court and fined. Hosts were often horrified by the bedraggled state and ill health of slum children, while the children themselves were taken aback by primitive rural conditions and their first sight of farm animals. Although many suffered emotionally from being wrenched from their families, for most the evacuation was an adventure.

BRITAIN AT WAR WITH GERMANY

"This morning the British Ambassador in Berlin handed the German Government a final note stating that, unless we heard from them by eleven o'clock that they were prepared at once to withdraw their troops from Poland, a state of war would exist between us. I have to tell you now that no such undertaking has been received, and that consequently this country is at war with Germany ... Now may God bless you all and may He defend the right. For it is evil things that we shall be fighting against, brute force, bad faith, injustice, oppression, and persecution. And against them I am certain that the right will prevail."
Neville Chamberlain, radio broadcast, September 3, 1939

War at sea

"I shall face my fate with firm faith in the cause and the future of the nation and of my Führer."

Captain Hans Langsdorff, in a letter to his wife, December 19, 1939

On the day war was declared, the German submarine U-30 torpedoed the liner *Athenia* on her way from Glasgow to Montreal—without warning. The ship sank with the loss of 112 passengers and crew. Twenty-eight of them were US citizens. Nevertheless, within hours President Roosevelt had announced that his government was preparing "a declaration of American neutrality."

By the end of September 1939, twenty British ships had been sunk by U-boats. On October 16, the battleship *Royal Oak* was torpedoed near her home base of Scapa Flow with the loss of 800 men. Meanwhile, the Germans were deploying magnetic mines in the North Sea, which sunk five British ships and several foreign vessels, including one neutral Dutch merchantman with the loss of 140 lives.

FAIR GAME

At the beginning of the war, U-boats were supposed to obey international laws governing the conduct of war at sea. As part of the Hague Conventions, these allowed merchant ships to be stopped and searched. If they were found to be carrying enemy cargo, they could be sunk, but only after the crew had been seen safely into lifeboats. However, on February 20, 1940, Hitler declared all shipping to be fair game—neutral as well as Allied. Neutral ships passing through the English Channel had been putting into British ports to have their cargo checked and pick up a certificate saying that they were not carrying any contraband on its way to Germany. Hitler hoped his threat would force neutral countries to divert cargos to German ports, robbing Britain of valuable trade. Otherwise, all neutral vessels were to be treated as suspicious and U-boat commanders were ordered to open fire without warning. Merely sailing in a zig-zag pattern would be taken as grounds for torpedoing.

Hunting in "wolf packs," German U-boats attempted to put a stranglehold on Britain, sinking shipping bound for its ports in what became known as the Battle of the Atlantic. For Britain the situation became more perilous after France had fallen and German submarines could sail from bases along the French coast.

BATTLE OF THE RIVER PLATE

The German surface fleet suffered reverses from the outset in World War II. On December 13, 1939, the pocket battleship *Admiral Graf Spee* was cornered in the River Plate by three British cruisers. In the ensuing battle the *Admiral Graf Spee* put into Montevideo for repairs. Forced to leave port four days later, the pride of the German navy was scuttled just outside the harbor.

The 10,000-ton pocket battleship *Admiral Graf Spee*—her size having been limited under the Versailles Treaty—was at sea when war was declared in 1939. After hostilities began, her Captain, Hans Langsdorff, received orders that he was to sink British merchant ships, but to avoid combat with superior enemy forces. That autumn, the *Admiral Graf Spee* sank nine merchant ships in the South Atlantic and Indian Ocean. Langsdorff strictly adhered to the rules of maritime war and not a life was lost in these sinkings. The captured crews were transferred to the supply ship *Altmark*—which was later stopped in Norwegian waters by HMS *Cossack* and 303 British seamen freed.

German sailors on deck
A U-boat travels above water during a lull on patrol, 1940.

A MATTER OF HONOR

"After a long and inward struggle, I reached the grave decision to scuttle the Panzerschiff Graf Spee in order that she should not fall into the hands of the enemy. I am convinced that under the circumstances this decision was the only one I could make after I had taken my ship into the trap of Montevideo. With the ammunition remaining, any attempt to break out to open and deep water was bound to fail. … I decided from the beginning to bear the consequences involved in this decision."
Captain Hans Langsdorff, note to the German ambassador to Buenos Aires, December 19, 1939

HUNTING GROUPS

The Royal Navy formed nine hunting groups—totaling three battleships, two battlecruisers, four aircraft carriers, and sixteen cruisers—to look for the *Admiral Graf Spee*. On December 13, the cruiser HMS *Exeter* and the light cruisers *Ajax* and *Achilles* located her near the coast of South America, and the Battle of the River Plate ensued. During the battle, the *Exeter* was badly damaged, but her eight-inch guns had already inflicted crippling damage to the *Admiral Graf Spee*. Repairs could not be made at sea and, unable to outrun her attackers, the *Admiral Graf Spee* put into Montevideo, Uruguay. Langsdorff was granted permission to remain in port for four days. Meanwhile, the Royal Navy called up reinforcements. In fact, only the *Cumberland* arrived. But fearing a larger force awaited him, when Langsdorff left port he gave orders to his crew to scuttle the ship.

DEATH OF THE CAPTAIN

Captain Langsdorff and some of his crew reached Buenos Aires, Argentina, where they were to be interned. After sending a note of explanation to the German ambassador and writing letters to his wife and parents, Langsdorff wrapped himself in the flag he had taken from the *Admiral Graf Spee*, put a pistol to his head, and pulled the trigger. The first shot grazed the back of his head. A second, through the forehead, killed him.

1940–Timeline

1940

THE AXIS ADVANCES

BRITAIN AND FRANCE COULD DO LITTLE ABOUT THE
SITUATION IN POLAND, SO THE WAR WAS LARGELY
CONFINED TO THE SEA AND TO PROPAGANDA FOR THE
FIRST FEW MONTHS OF 1940. HOWEVER, BY THE END OF THE
YEAR, WESTERN EUROPE WOULD HAVE BEEN OVERRUN.
BRITAIN—AND ITS EMPIRE—WOULD STAND ALONE AGAINST
THE MIGHT OF THE THIRD REICH, WHILE BOMBS RAINED
DOWN ON LONDON AND ITS OTHER MAJOR CITIES.

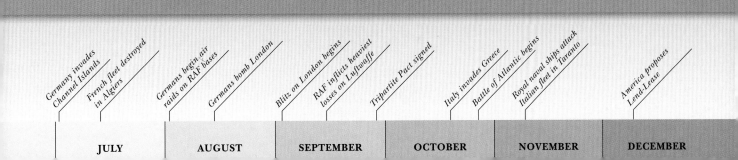

Germany invades
Channel Islands

French fleet destroyed
in Algiers

Germans begin air
raids on RAF bases

Germans bomb London

Blitz on London begins

RAF inflicts heaviest
losses on Luftwaffe

Tripartite Pact signed

Italy invades Greece

Battle of Atlantic begins

Royal naval ships attack
Italian fleet in Taranto

America proposes
Lend-Lease

| JULY | AUGUST | SEPTEMBER | OCTOBER | NOVEMBER | DECEMBER |

The period between September 1939 and May 1940 was called the Phony War or the Bore War, a pun on the Boer War of 1899–1902. Winston Churchill—since September 4, 1939 back in the cabinet as First Sea Lord—called it the Twilight War. The Germans called it the *Sitzkrieg*, or "sitting war"; the French *drôle de guerre*, or "funny war"; the Italians *la guerra fittiza* or *la finta guerra*—the "fictitious war" or "false war." For seven months, nothing much seemed to happen.

AIR RAIDS EXPECTED

The British government had expected 100,000 casualties in the first few weeks of the war due to air raids. Hospital beds had been cleared. Mortuaries were stacked with cardboard coffins, and lime-pits were dug to dispose of the dead. Every home had a stirrup pump and a long-handled shovel to deal with incendiary bombs. Before identity cards could be issued, everyone in Britain was urged to carry a luggage label with their name and address on it, in case they were killed or badly wounded. A night-time blackout was enforced with Air Raid Wardens yelling "Put that light out!" and issuing heavy fines. Shops sold out of blackout curtains and windows had to be painted black instead. Railroad cars were illuminated by an eerie blue light. There was chaos on the unlit buses and regulations on car headlamps had to be relaxed, allowing a two-inch-wide beam from one headlamp, after road accidents soared. And West End theaters that had been closed at the beginning of the war were reopened to raise morale.

Homeless (ABOVE)

Two women inspect the bombed-out wreckage of the almshouse in which they lived, Berkshire, England, 1939.

Civil defense (ABOVE)

Sandbag defenses are erected to protect Birmingham City Hall, England, 1939.

TROOP MOVEMENTS

Meanwhile, there had been troop movements. The French manned the Maginot Line, the defensive fortification that faced Germany's Siegfried Line, which was designed to repulse an attack similar to the one the Germans had made at the beginning of World War I. The first Canadian troops turned up in Britain and 158,000 British soldiers (the British Expeditionary Force, or BEF) landed in France. Hitler escaped a bomb blast in the Munich bierkeller where he made his traditional speech on the anniversary of the 1923 putsch. He was furious at Britain and France for turning down another peace offer.

NO DEAL

In 1940, the waiting would be over. Hitler would launch his Blitzkrieg in the west. By the end of the year, only Britain and her Empire would stand in the way of Hitler's global ambitions. Much as Hitler would have liked to make peace with Britain, allowing it to maintain its great maritime Empire while he expanded his land empire on the European continent, one indomitable force stood in his way—the willpower of Winston Churchill, who had been implacably opposed to Hitler since 1932.

British inspection (LEFT)

A pillbox—a small concrete hut for a machine gun—on the Maginot Line is reviewed by British officers, France, 1939.

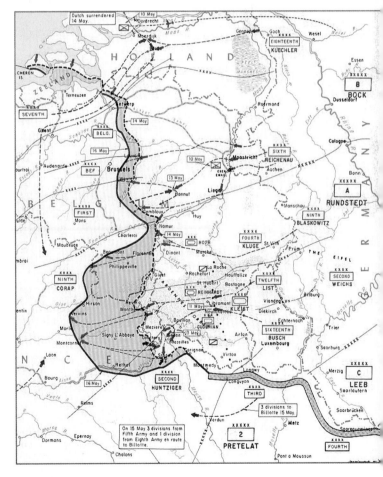

Northwestern France (ABOVE)

The campaign in the west as the Germans rapidly advance into France, May 16, 1940.

Blitzkrieg

"The supreme leadership must decide whether my objective is to be Amiens or Paris. In my opinion, the correct course is to drive past Amiens and on to the English Channel."

General Heinz Guderian

Britain and France were not prepared for Blitzkrieg. Although they had pioneered tank warfare in World War I, they were still mired in the thinking of 1918. The French imagined that the Germans could be stopped by the fortified Maginot Line. The British were ready to dig in, in a new trench line. But the Germans had developed a new "lightning" form of warfare, using aircraft and fast-moving armored columns to cut through enemy lines.

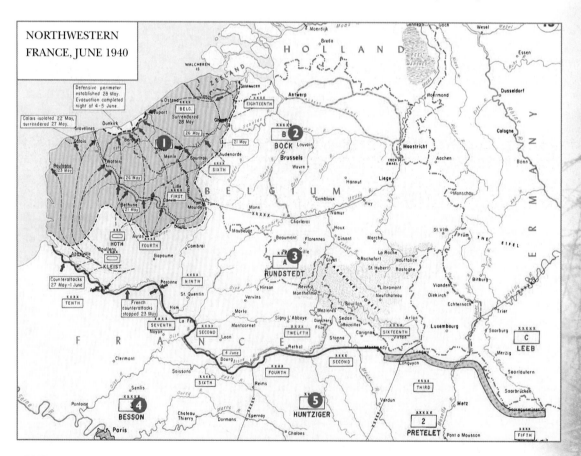

NORTHWESTERN FRANCE, JUNE 1940

POSITION OF ARMIES

1 *British Expeditionary Force (BEF)*
2 *Bock (Germany)*
3 *Rundstedt (Germany)*
4 *Besson (France)*
5 *Huntziger (France)*

Invasion of the Netherlands (LEFT)
Paratroopers descend on The Hague as German troops sweep towards Amsterdam, the Netherlands, 1940.

Nowhere to go (LEFT)
Belgian refugees walk past the ruins of houses and towns, Belgium, 1942.

Battle for France (BELOW)
German soldiers advance while under fire, France, 1940.

The battle for France

"We have been defeated … We are beaten; we have lost the battle … The front is broken near Sedan."

French Prime Minister Paul Reynaud, phone call to Winston Churchill, May 17, 1940

The Allies had imagined that the main German attack on France would come through Liège and Namur as it had in World War I. This was perfect tank country. Instead, on May 10, the Germans sent 1,500,000 men and over 1,500 tanks—two-thirds of Germany's forces in the west and nearly three-quarters of its tanks—through the Ardennes Forest, which the French had thought impassable to armor.

The German attack hit the weakest part of the front, defended by just twelve infantry divisions and four cavalry divisions mounted on horseback. German tanks reached France in fewer than three days, crossing the border on the evening of May 12. The infantry followed, using pathways through the woods, traveling so fast that they reached the River Meuse just a day behind the armor. Not expecting an advance in that area, the French defenses were rudimentary, with few anti-aircraft or anti-tank guns. On May 13, after the French defenders were devastated by dive bombers, German infantry crossed the Meuse, followed by the tanks. On May 15, they broke through what remained of the French defenses and it was estimated that, at that rate, the Germans could be in Paris in two days.

"SICKLE STROKE"

Instead, the Germans turned westward toward the Channel, covering almost 50 miles of open country in a day. The advance was so fast that even the German High Command were worried that it was vulnerable to attack. However, French resistance collapsed. The Panzers then turned northward toward Calais in a move known as the *Sichelschitt*, or "sickle stroke." This split Allied forces. Those that had advanced into Belgium were now threatened with encirclement. On May 21, the British commander, Viscount Gort, launched an attack southward against the Germans' right flank in an attempt to break through.

Tank capture (LEFT)
A French tank crew surrenders to a German infantry unit, France, 1940.

Further into France (RIGHT)
German troops storm a burning farmhouse during the invasion of France, 1940.

HIATUS

By that time, Boulogne and Calais had fallen. Dunkirk was now the only Channel port left in Allied hands through which the British Expeditionary Force (BEF) could withdraw. But when the Germans reached the outskirts, Hitler ordered them to halt. News of Gort's counterattack was confused and the British seemed a genuine threat. But Gort did not have the armor to break through. Short of supplies and ammunition, on May 25 he ordered the BEF to fall back on Dunkirk. Hitler then ordered the advance on Dunkirk be resumed. But the hiatus had allowed the British to consolidate their defenses.

LETTER FROM ROMMEL TO HIS WIFE

"Dearest Lu,
I have come up for breath for the first time today and have a moment to write. Everything wonderful so far. Am way ahead of my neighbors. I'm completely hoarse from orders and shouting. Had a bare three hours' sleep and an occasional meal. Otherwise I'm absolutely fine. Make do with this, please, I'm too tired for more …"
Panzer leader Erwin Rommel, letter to his wife, May 11, 1940

Dunkirk

"The beaches were full of troops. We couldn't move, we just had to dig in and wait. We had no idea what was happening. There was no food and we thought we were going to starve."

Ivan Daunt, the Queen's Own Royal West Kent Regiment

With the British Expeditionary Force (BEF) falling back on Dunkirk, the Luftwaffe began bombing the harbor, putting it out of action. On May 19, the Royal Navy was ordered to prepare for an evacuation. In Britain, owners of motorized pleasure craft were told to report to the Admiralty. The race to evacuate the troops from the beaches before Dunkirk fell to the Germans was now on.

Cover from RAF fighters based in England prevented Luftwaffe leader Herman Göring fulfilling his boast that he could destroy what was left of the BEF with his planes alone. Hitler had also decided to reserve the Panzers for use against the remains of the French Army to the south. Dunkirk's bomb-damaged breakwater was still serviceable, allowing many of the troops to be taken off by larger craft. The rest were picked up

Escaping Dunkirk (BELOW)
British troops return fire at attacking planes while evacuating the beach at Dunkirk, France, 1940.

directly from a ten-mile stretch of beach by small craft largely manned by amateur sailors. In all, 848 British, French, and Belgian ships of all sizes—from destroyers to private motor cruisers—joined the operation. In the eight days of the evacuation, some 340,000 men, two-thirds of them British, were rescued. But almost all their equipment was abandoned and, of the 41 destroyers participating in the evacuation, six were sunk and 19 others damaged. Another 220,000 Allied troops were rescued by British ships from Cherbourg, St. Malo, Brest, and St. Nazaire in northwestern France, bringing the total of Allied troops evacuated to about 560,000. But in three weeks the German Army had taken more than one million men prisoner.

The "little ships" (RIGHT)
A number of the small craft, pleasure yachts, and dinghies that helped evacuate the BEF at Dunkirk, 1940.

"VICTORY" AT DUNKIRK

Although the action at Dunkirk was actually a withdrawal, it was hailed as a victory by the British. In the long run, it proved decisive. The majority of Britain's most experienced troops had been saved. Controversy still rages about why Hitler stayed his hand and allowed the British Army to get away. It was one of the several key mistakes he made during World War II. Some believe that Hitler still wanted to make peace with Britain and thought that this might be more easily achieved if the British Army was not forced into a humiliating surrender.

BOMBING ON THE BEACH

"Eventually we got down to the beach at Dunkirk and there were blokes lying all over who'd been killed. You were such an easy target. There was such a concentration of fire by the enemy and we were so tightly packed that they couldn't really miss. We built a trench, but with no ships to take us off we stayed there for three days, while they were bombing and shelling."
Sergeant Harry Garrett, Royal Artillery

The collapse of France

"But has the last word been said? Must hope disappear? Is defeat final? No! Believe me, I speak to you with full knowledge of the facts and tell you that nothing is lost for France."

Charles de Gaulle, BBC broadcast, June 18, 1940

Although the BEF was now safely back in Britain, the Battle of France was not over. The French had lost 30 divisions so far but they could still muster 49 divisions, along with another 17 who were still holding the Maginot Line. But the Germans had 140 divisions at their disposal, including ten divisions of tanks.

On June 5, the Wehrmacht started pushing southward from their positions on the Somme. The French held them for two days, but on June 7 Panzers under Major-General Erwin Rommel broke through southwestward toward Rouen. Two days after that they crossed the River Seine. That same day, June 9, the Germans broke through to the southeast and made a dash for the Swiss border, cutting off the French forces still holding the Maginot Line. To all intents and purposes, the Battle of France was lost.

ITALY JOINS THE WAR

Until then, the British had hoped that Italy might be persuaded to join the Allied side, as it had in World War I, or at least remain neutral. However, on June 10, 1940, Benito Mussolini declared war on France and Great Britain. Some 30 Italian divisions massed on the French frontier, though the attack was delayed until June 20. Even then the Italians made little progress against local defenses and no contributions of strategic importance.

THE FRENCH GOVERNMENT FALLS

As the Germans advanced, the French government under Paul Reynaud had left Paris for Cangé, near Tours. There, on June 12, Reynaud received news that the Battle of France was lost. He wanted to continue the war from the French possessions in North Africa, but his cabinet was split. On June 14, 1940, the Germans entered Paris and drove on rapidly south. The French government had to flee south from Tours to Bordeaux to stay ahead of the German advance. The French Army was now split into a dozen fragments and its commander General Maxime Weygand pressed for an armistice. Reynaud's position was untenable and he resigned on June 16. He was replaced by the elderly Marshal Philippe Pétain, France's most honored soldier in World War I and hero of the Battle of Verdun.

PÉTAIN AND DE GAULLE

On June 16, the day Marshal Philippe Pétain took over the government of France, General Charles de Gaulle, a former tank commander and undersecretary for defense in Paul Reynaud's recently fallen French government, arrived in London. He was determined to overturn the humiliation the French nation had suffered, falling so swiftly to the German onslaught.

On the night de Gaulle arrived in London, Marshall Pétain's government asked for an armistice. While the two sides discussed terms, the German advance continued, swallowing two-thirds of the country. On June 22, 1940, the representatives of Germany and France met at Compiègne, Picardy, northeastern France, in the same railroad carriage where the armistice ending World War I was signed. There, Pétain signed the surrender while Hitler looked on. France was to be divided into two zones. The northern part of France from the Swiss border to the Channel and a western strip down the Atlantic coast to the Spanish border was to be held under German military occupation. The rump of the country was to be left in the hands of a collaborationist government under Pétain based at Vichy in south-central France.

But all was not lost. On June 18, de Gaulle began broadcasting appeals for France to continue the war from London, where he organized the Free French Forces. On

August 2, 1940, he was tried *in absentia* by a French military court and sentenced to death. Four years later, he would return to France a national hero.

THE FATE OF THE FRENCH FLEET

Still in control of the seas, the British government decided that it could not risk the French Navy at its naval base in Algeria falling into German hands. On July 3, 1940, ships of the Royal Navy appeared off the Algerian coast. When the French fleet refused to join the Allies, the British opened fire, putting the fleet out of action. In protest the Vichy government broke diplomatic relations with the British. The ships that survived were later destroyed by the Germans to prevent them falling into Allied hands. For the moment though, the British had to suffer another humiliation. On July 1, German forces landed on the Channel Islands, the only part of Britain to be occupied during the war.

DE GAULLE CALLS FOR RESISTANCE

"The destiny of the world is here. I, General de Gaulle, currently in London, invite the officers and the French soldiers who are located in British territory or who would come there, with their weapons or without their weapons. I invite the engineers and the special workers of armament industries who are located in British territory or who would come there, to put themselves in contact with me. Whatever happens, the flame of the French resistance must not be extinguished and will not be extinguished."
Charles de Gaulle, BBC broadcast,
June 18, 1940

The fall of Paris
German troops and artillery parade down the Champs-Élysées from the Arc de Triomphe, Paris, France, 1940.

The Home Guard

"In addition to Regulars and Territorials, twelve divisions of equal quality to that of the International Brigade in Spain ... formed the same way, by voluntary enlistment from amongst ex-servicemen and youths."

Captain Tom Wintringham,
Head of the Home Guard Training School, Osterley Park, London

After the fall of France, Britain expected to be invaded. Even Churchill believed that, in the face of a Nazi onslaught, it would not expect to hold out for more than a few weeks. However, it was vital, in his view, that the country should put up a fight, so a new force was mustered.

On May 14, 1940, four days after the Blitzkrieg in Western Europe had started, Secretary of State for War Anthony Eden went on the BBC to make an appeal. "We want large numbers of such men in Great Britain who are British subjects, between the ages of 17 and 65, to come forward now and offer their services in order to make assurance [that any invasion would fail] doubly sure," he said. "The name of the new force which is now to be raised will be the Local Defense Volunteers. This name describes its duties in three words. You will not be paid, but you will receive uniforms and will be armed." The government was expecting 150,000 men to volunteer. Within the first month, 750,000 men had volunteered, and by the end of June, 1940, the total number of volunteers was over one million. Impressed, on August 23, 1940, Churchill renamed the volunteer force the Home Guard.

ILL-EQUIPPED

The Home Guard were to delay an enemy invasion force and to give the British Army time to form a proper defensive line. The Home Guard were expected to take on highly trained, well-armed German troops. However, as all modern weapons were given to the regular forces, they were armed only with shotguns, air rifles, old hunting rifles, museum pieces, and pieces of gas-pipe with knives welded to the end. Later they were issued weapons of World War I vintage, and US and Canadian rifles whose ammunition was not interchangeable. They were trained to defend Britain against landings of paratroopers. Then, as the danger of invasion receded, they were used as aircraft observers and in coastal defense patrols.

WEAPONS AND UNIFORM

"I was fourteen years old at the time and lived at Drury Lane, before going into the army at seventeen and a half. Through the day I worked as a vanboy in Smithfield meat market. When I first joined with my bicycle, the only weapons we had were pikes, which were nearly twice my height. Later we got the American P14 rifle, and later still got a Piat gun. We also got a lot of training from the Hampshire Regiment. Before I got my uniform I just had a forage cap with the Royal Fusiliers badge and an LDV armband, later we got issued with just denims before khaki issue."
George Burton, Home Guard

Volunteer training (RIGHT)
Local Defense Volunteers practice a marching drill, using sticks in place of rifles, in Doncaster, England, 1940.

The Home Guard (LEFT)
*Winston Churchill inspects a brigade of the
Home Guard in Spencer's Yard, London.*

The Battle of Britain

"Never in the field of human conflict was so much owed by so many to so few."

Winston Churchill, House of Commons, August 20, 1940

With France under the Nazi heel, Hitler turned his attention to Britain. Peace overtures were once again rebuffed by Churchill. So German plans went ahead for "Operation Sealion"—the invasion of Britain. The date was set for August 25, 1940. But to defeat the Royal Navy in the Channel and land German troops on British beaches, the Luftwaffe had first to win the battle in the skies.

On August 1, 1940, Hitler ordered his airforce to smash the RAF in the air and on the ground. German planes flew from Norway and Denmark, Belgium and Holland, and northern France. In all the Luftwaffe had 2,442 aircraft—1,305 bombers and 1,137 fighters. The RAF had just 620 fighters, but production was slowly rising. The RAF also had a shortage of trained pilots, but they were joined by Polish and Czech pilots who had escaped from Eastern Europe. Although the German Messerschmitt Bf 109E fighter plane was faster than the British Hurricane, the Spitfire, though in short supply, was unrivalled as an interceptor. German bombers were vulnerable, particularly as their protecting fighter planes were at the limit of their range. The British also had an advanced radar defense network, capable of issuing warnings of incoming German planes and directing counterattacks by radio.

ATTACK ON BERLIN

By early August the Germans were sending across the Channel up to 1,500 aircraft a day. Although the RAF inflicted heavy losses, by late August the Luftwaffe was close to winning the air war. British radar stations and operations centers were being bombed, and so aircraft were being destroyed on the ground. Airfields were pitted with bomb craters and it was becoming difficult to coordinate formations in the air. Exhausted British pilots were seeing action several times a day. Fifteen to twenty experienced pilots were being killed or wounded every day. British Fighter Command was reaching its last gasp and salvation came only by accident. Late in the evening of August 24, a German plane accidentally bombed civilian targets in

London. Winston Churchill immediately ordered a retaliatory attack on Berlin. The next night, 81 bombers took off for the German capital. Only 29 planes made it, the rest having got lost on the way. The damage to Berlin was slight but an infuriated Adolf Hitler switched German attacks from the RAF's airfields to the terror bombing of London.

Enemy incoming (BELOW)
Responding to an air raid warning, RAF pilots scramble towards their planes.

Hurricane squadron (ABOVE)

*A squadron of Hawker Hurricanes flies in tight
formation, practicing for an aerial display.*

St. Paul's unscathed (LEFT)
London's St. Paul's Cathedral remains intact in the fire-bomb raid of December 29, 1940.

Battling the blaze (BELOW)
London firefighters struggle to contain the firestorm produced by German bombardment on December 29, 1940.

The Blitz

"If they send over a hundred bombers to bomb our cities … then we shall send a thousand planes to bomb theirs. And if they think that they can destroy our cities … then we shall wipe theirs from the face of the earth."

Adolf Hitler

Hitler's terror bombing of London and Britain's other major cities from September 1940 to May 1941 was called the Blitz. Over 43,000 civilians were killed, 137,000 injured, and more than a million houses destroyed or damaged. Despite the terrible suffering, it gave British Fighter Command the breathing space to recover and, ultimately, win the war in the air.

The Blitz began late in the afternoon of September 7, when 364 German bombers, escorted by 515 fighters, attacked the Port of London and London's East End. Another 133 bombers attacked that night, guided by the fires. Many of the bombs aimed at the docks fell on neighboring residential areas. Raids on London continued for 57 consecutive nights. Anti-aircraft guns were largely ineffective, but continued firing to maintain morale. On October 15, in the worst air raid so far, 400 bombers dropped their bombs on London. Others bombed Birmingham and Bristol, with the RAF's 41 defenders downing just one Heinkel bomber. Later, Coventry, Southampton, Liverpool, Glasgow, Swindon, Plymouth, Cardiff, Manchester, Sheffield, Portsmouth, and Avonmouth were bombed. On December 29, a massive attack with incendiaries and high-explosive bombs on the City of London caused what has been called "The Second Great Fire of London." The city was only saved from being destroyed in a firestorm when bad weather in Germany prevented another wave of bombers taking off.

INVASION POSTPONED

However, as the RAF began to recover, the odds turned in their favor. They began shooting down bombers faster than German factories could produce them. Even so, Hitler continued his preparations for Operation Sealion, though its start date was repeatedly postponed until winter conditions in the Channel made an invasion impossible. The Luftwaffe switched to night bombing, which was much less effective militarily. By then the Battle of Britain was over. Fighter Command had denied the Germans victory in the air that would have led to the invasion of Britain. By the time the weather was suitable for an invasion the following spring, Hitler had turned his eyes eastward toward the USSR.

EYEWITNESS ACCOUNT OF THE BLITZ

"Into the dark shadowed spaces below us, while we watched, whole batches of incendiary bombs fell. We saw two dozen go off in two seconds. They flashed terrifically, then quickly simmered down to pin points of dazzling white, burning ferociously … Soon a yellow flame would leap up from the white center. They had done their work—another building was on fire … The greatest of all the fires was directly in front of us. Flames seemed to whip hundreds of feet into the air. Pinkish-white smoke ballooned upward in a great cloud, and out of this cloud there gradually took shape—so faintly at first that we weren't sure we saw correctly—the gigantic dome of St. Paul's Cathedral."
Ernie Pyle, roving correspondent for Scripps Howard News Service

Lend-lease

"Here is the answer I will give President Roosevelt …

Give us the tools and we will finish the job."

Winston Churchill, BBC broadcast, February 9, 1941

Although the US remained determinedly isolationist, it found itself being inexorably drawn into the war. Japan was flexing its muscles in the Pacific. There were Fascist sympathizers in Latin America. The Soviet Union was no friend. If Britain fell, America would find itself surrounded. The answer was to support the United Kingdom materially, through lend-lease.

In 1935, Congress passed a Neutrality Act with the specific intention of keeping the US out of any future European war. Other laws sought to minimize involvement with the belligerent nations. While abiding by the law, President Roosevelt warned that America would inevitably be menaced by the dictatorial nations—Germany, Italy, and Japan. He proposed quarantining aggressor nations, but when he threatened to cut off diplomatic relations the American people grew alarmed. In December 1937, the Japanese sank the American gunboat USS *Panay* on the River Yangtze in China. It was feared that this would spark war, but Roosevelt accepted Japanese apologies. When World War II broke out in Europe in September 1939, Roosevelt persuaded Congress to amend the neutrality acts to allow Britain and France to buy arms on a "cash and carry" basis. After the fall of France, he convinced Congress to send Britain "all aid short of war"—even providing 50 old destroyers in exchange for eight naval bases.

PASSED BY CONGRESS

By the summer of 1940, Britain was running out of cash, so in December Roosevelt proposed the idea of "lend-lease." The Lend-Lease Act was passed by Congress in March 1941. This allowed the President to aid any nation that he considered was vital to the defense of the US in return for any "direct or indirect benefit which the President deems satisfactory." While most aid went to Britain and the Commonwealth countries, it was later extended to China and the Soviet Union, after they were attacked. Some $50 billion in aid—sometimes as outright gifts—was provided this way, while US troops stationed abroad received some $8 billion in aid from host nations.

Lend–lease ships (LEFT)

Examples of the 50 old-fashioned destroyers provided by the US Navy to aid the British war effort, 1940.

US neutrality questioned (RIGHT)

Franklin Delano Roosevelt broadcasts to the American people to explain continued American neutrality as the war in Europe escalates.

ROOSEVELT BUILDS UP DEFENSES

"I want to make it clear that it is the purpose of the nation to build now with all possible speed every machine, every arsenal, every factory that we need to manufacture our defense material. We have the men, the skill, the wealth, and above all, the will … As planes and ships and guns and shells are produced, your government, with its defense experts, can then determine how best to use them to defend this hemisphere. The decision as to how much shall be sent abroad and how much shall remain at home must be made on the basis of our overall military necessities. We must be the great arsenal of democracy."

Franklin Delano Roosevelt, radio "Fireside Chat," December 29, 1940

Italy on the march

"The course of the war against England was not decided at Dunkirk. It became clear in Berlin that it could only be brought to a rapid conclusion by two major operations: by a German landing in England and by the Italian offensive against the Suez Canal."

Colonel Heinz Hegenreiner, German liaison officer to Marshal Graziani

Since Italy had joined the war on June 10, 1940, it had made few territorial gains. Its army had not done well against the French, but it already had a foothold in the Balkans after taking Albania in April 1939. Hitler showed no interest in the region, so Mussolini decided to extend the Italian Empire eastward.

ITALY INVADES GREECE

In preparation for his attack on the Soviet Union, Hitler began drawing other Central European countries—Hungary, Romania, Slovakia, Bulgaria, Yugoslavia—into the Axis. Following Germany's huge gains in the west, Italy began to

War in the desert
An Italian tank at rest in the sands of northern Eygypt, 1940.

find itself very much the junior partner in the Pact of Steel. Mussolini wanted to make some territorial gains of his own. So without informing Hitler, on October 28, 1940, he sent 155,000 men across the Albanian border into Greece. The Italian invasion was a disaster. Mussolini's seven divisions were halted by a handful of Greeks, who pushed the Italians back until, by mid-December, the Greeks occupied one third of Albania.

HITLER HELPS OUT

The British rallied to the defense of Greece, sending men and planes to airbases on the mainland near Athens. This put them within striking distance of the Romanian oilfields at Ploiesti, which were vital to Germany's attack on the USSR. So Hitler had no option but to help Mussolini out. In March 1941, there was a *coup d'état* against the pro-Axis regime in Belgrade, so the Germans and Italians decided to invade Yugoslavia and sweep through into Greece. They made a lightning thrust through the Balkans, forcing the British to evacuate their forces from mainland Greece, though 20,000 remained as prisoners of war. By May 11, the whole of Greece and the Aegean islands, with the exception of Crete, were in German hands.

THE ITALIAN INVASION OF EGYPT REPULSED

After the fall of France in 1940, Mussolini feared that Hitler would make peace with the British. Any pact between Britain and Germany would thwart Mussolini's territorial ambitions in the Mediterranean. The armistice signed at Compiègne on June 22, 1940, was a disappointment. Mussolini coveted the French possessions in North Africa, but they remained in the hands of the Vichy government.

Italy already had one possession in North Africa—Libya, which it had invaded in 1911. By the outbreak of World War II, some 150,000 Italian colonists lived there. So when the British rejected Hitler's peace overtures, Mussolini turned his attention to Egypt, which had been in British hands since 1882. He ordered his commander in North Africa, Marshal Rudolfo Graziani, to launch an offensive eastward against the British troops in Egypt who were under the command of General Sir Archibald Wavell. On September 13, 1940, the Italian Tenth Army took the small border port of Sollum. They then advanced a further 50 miles into Egypt and occupied the British base at Sidi Barrani on September 16. Twelve weeks later the British Western Desert Force under Lieutenant-General Richard O'Connor started a "five-day raid," which pushed the Italians back across the border on December 10.

GERMAN VICTORY PARADE IN ATHENS

"The population of Athens had fully grasped the significance of the historical hour though by no means were all of the captured soldiers of the brave Greek army released or sent home. Without arms, but erect, these men mingled with the field-gray of the Germans and the thousands of Greek civilians. Yesterday's enemies—a motley, southerly, excitable crowd of people—are full of anticipation. Strange as it may sound, it was really hard to imagine that, despite the number of soldiers in field-gray, war has just passed over this country and that we, in the eyes of the Athenians, had originally come as enemies. But no shot was heard, no bomb fell and no stone was dislodged in this metropolis … absolutely no animosity existed between the victor and the vanquished. On the contrary, full harmony and mutual respect prevailed. Gay anticipation is reflected in the faces of the spectators."
General Julius Ringel at the German victory parade in Athens, May 5, 1941

TOBRUK

Reinforced by Australian troops, the Western Desert Force continued the advance and took the small port of Tobruk in northeast Libya on January 21, 1941. By the time the Italians surrendered on February 7, the British had driven them back 500 miles, taking over 130,000 prisoners along with 400 tanks and 1,290 guns. Meeting no further resistance, the Western Desert Force could have gone on to take Tripoli, but their supply lines were already overstretched and Churchill wanted to divert men and resources to Greece. Once again, Hitler came to Mussolini's aid and sent in the Afrika Korps, which prolonged the fighting in North Africa for another three years.

War in the Atlantic

"The only thing that ever frightened me during the war was the U-boat peril."

Winston Churchill

Great Britain is a small island. Cut off from the European Continent, now in Nazi hands, it had to be supplied via the Atlantic by ships from North America, the West Indies, southern Africa, and its colonies in the Far East. If Germany could break that supply line, Britain was doomed.

Until the fall of France, the British and French managed to drive German merchant shipping from the Atlantic, while the Royal Navy kept the German Navy, or *Kriegsmarine*, largely blockaded in its Baltic ports. However, the Royal Navy suffered significant losses off Norway and Dunkirk, while the French Navy was lost to the Allies. The US helped out by supplying the British with 50 old destroyers in exchange for bases in Bermuda, Newfoundland, and the Caribbean. But the conquest of Norway and France gave the Germans forward bases. At the same time Italian air and sea power threatened shipping coming through Suez, forcing British merchantmen from the Far East to take the longer route around the Cape of Good Hope.

THE "HAPPY TIME"

Guided by long-range reconnaissance, German U-boats and armed surface raiders disguised as merchant ships succeeded in sinking three million tons of Allied shipping between the fall of France and the end of 1940. German submariners called this the "happy time." The British had developed Asdic—later known as sonar—to detect submarines underwater, but U-boats simply stayed away from British convoys and their escorts during the day and attacked, on the surface, at night. The British beefed up the Royal Navy's escort capability by introducing corvettes, small, fast warships of less than 1,000 tons. The Royal Canadian Navy, which was small in 1939, soon grew big

enough to fill the breach. The US, although remaining neutral, began to behave in a most un-neutral fashion. It occupied Greenland and Iceland, which belonged to German-occupied Denmark, giving Britain vital mid-Atlantic bases. From May 1941, the US Navy took over escort duties in the western Atlantic. Then on October 30, 1941, the USS *Reuben James* was torpedoed and sunk by the German submarine U-562. But even this was not enough to convince US isolationists that America had to join the war.

PERSONAL HYGIENE ON A U-BOAT

"On board I found it best to bear all the privations with good humor and forget the usual day-to-day comforts of life, like washing hands and face, taking a hot shower, brushing teeth, and shaving. During operations in the Atlantic or Arctic one simply could not escape becoming encrusted with dirt. At first, I thought a man could get scabies or some other skin disease if he didn't wash down at least once a day. To my surprise, I soon learned that we could make do by just rinsing off our hands a couple of times a week with salt water. Afterwards, we splashed 'Cologne 4711' onto our faces and distributed any remaining dirt with ointment ... and sprinkled birch water to neutralize the odor, which seemed to differ with each man."
Otto Giese, U-boat veteran

Depth-charge blast
An experimental depth charge is dropped and detonated by HMS Wessex, *1938.*

The Tripartite Pact

"The pact is a military alliance between the three mightiest states of the world, comprising over 250 million people."

Joachim von Ribbentrop, Nazi foreign minister

With the war now going badly for the Allies, Germany, Italy, and Japan signed a new treaty called the Tripartite—or Three-Way—Pact. In it, they recognized each other's spheres of influence—Germany and Italy's in Europe, Japan's in "Greater East Asia." They agreed to assist one another if attacked. This was seen as an implicit warning to the US to stay neutral.

On September 27, 1940, Adolf Hitler, Italy's Foreign Minister Galeazzo Ciano, and Saburo Kurusu, representative of Imperial Japan, signed the Tripartite Pact in Berlin. The Pact recognized that a new order was being established in the world. Germany and Italy now controlled Europe, while Japan had established itself in Korea and China, and its Greater East Asian Empire would soon be expanding. The signatories undertook to assist each other if attacked by a power not already involved in the war in Europe or the Sino–Japanese war, and recognized the existing non-aggression pact that Germany had with the Soviet Union. Essentially, the only other significant power likely to intervene in the war was the United States.

The Tripartite Pact
Germany's Joachim von Ribbentrop, center, Japan's Saburo Kurusu, right, and Italy's Galeazzo Ciano, left, sign the pact in Berlin, Germany, 1940.

THE TRIPARTITE PACT BETWEEN JAPAN, GERMANY, AND ITALY, 1940

The Governments of Japan, Germany, and Italy consider it the prerequisite of a lasting peace that every nation in the world shall receive the space to which it is entitled. They have, therefore, decided to stand by and cooperate with one another in their efforts in the regions of Europe and Greater East Asia respectively. In doing this it is their prime purpose to establish and maintain a new order of things, calculated to promote the mutual prosperity and welfare of the peoples concerned. It is, furthermore, the desire of the three governments to extend cooperation to nations in other spheres of the world that are inclined to direct their efforts along lines similar to their own for the purpose of realizing their ultimate object, world peace. Accordingly, the governments of Japan, Germany, and Italy have agreed as follows:

ARTICLE 1. Japan recognizes and respects the leadership of Germany and Italy in the establishment of a new order in Europe.

ARTICLE 2. Germany and Italy recognize and respect the leadership of Japan in the establishment of a new order in Greater East Asia.

ARTICLE 3. Japan, Germany, and Italy agree to cooperate in their efforts on aforesaid lines. They further undertake to assist one another with all political, economic, and military means if *one of the Contracting Powers is attacked by a Power at present not involved in the European War or in the Japanese–Chinese conflict.*

ARTICLE 4. With a view to implementing the present pact, joint technical commissions, to be appointed by the respective governments of Japan, Germany, and Italy, will meet without delay.

ARTICLE 5. Japan, Germany, and Italy affirm that the above agreement affects in no way the political status existing at *present between each of the three Contracting Powers and Soviet Russia.*

ARTICLE 6. The present pact shall become valid immediately upon signature and shall remain in force ten years from the date on which it becomes effective. In due time, before the expiration of said term, the High Contracting Parties shall, at the request of any one of them, enter into negotiations for its renewal.

OTHER SIGNATORIES

The Tripartite Pact was subsequently joined by Hungary on November 20, 1940, Romania on November 23 and Slovakia on November 24, all of whom had Fascist governments. Pro-Nazi Bulgaria joined on March 1, 1941, before allowing German troops to pass through into Greece. Prince Paul, Regent of Yugoslavia, signed the Pact on March 25, 1941, but was overthrown by a military *coup d'état* supported by Britain. As the British could lend no immediate aid, the new government decided to abide by the provisions of the Pact, but Hitler invaded anyway. Just before the Axis powers signed the Pact, the Soviet Union was informed of its existence. Molotov flew to Berlin to discuss the possibility of joining. The Soviets wanted recognition of their annexation of Finland added, offering various economic incentives. But while it went through the motions, Germany had no intention of letting the Soviet Union join.

1941–Timeline

1941

GLOBAL WARFARE

AT THE BEGINNING OF 1941, BRITAIN STOOD BELEAGUERED.
GERMANY AND ITS ALLIES DOMINATED CONTINENTAL
EUROPE. BRITISH CITIES WERE BEING BOMBED NIGHTLY.
THE U-BOAT BLOCKADE THREATENED TO STARVE BRITAIN
INTO SURRENDER AND THE COUNTRY STILL FACED THE
IMMINENT DANGER OF INVASION. HOWEVER, BY THE END
OF THE YEAR, BRITAIN HAD TWO POWERFUL NEW ALLIES—
THE SOVIET UNION AND THE UNITED STATES.

Atlantic Charter

Arctic convoys set sail

British and Soviet
troops march into Iran

Siege of Leningrad begins

Japanese attack US
Navy at Pearl Harbor;
siege of Tobruk ends

US declares war on
Germany and Japan

| JULY | AUGUST | SEPTEMBER | OCTOBER | NOVEMBER | DECEMBER |

Although Britain faced its darkest hour in the winter months of 1941, its people were not downhearted. The RAF had won the Battle of Britain, proving that the Nazis and their Blitzkrieg tactics were not invincible. British and Australian troops had been making great strides against the Italians in North Africa. And now, at its head, Britain had the indomitable Winston Churchill, with his cigar, "V for Victory" sign, and his pugnacious looks that made him the personification of the "British bulldog." In June 1940, after the evacuation of Dunkirk, he had told the House of Commons: "We shall fight on the beaches, we shall fight on the landing grounds, we shall fight in the fields and in the streets, we shall fight in the hills; we shall never surrender …". The distinguished CBS correspondent, Edward R. Murrow, who broadcast from London throughout the Blitz, said of Churchill: "He mobilized the English language and sent it into battle to steady his fellow countrymen and hearten those Europeans upon whom the long dark night of tyranny had descended."

THIRD TERM

There was other good news for Britain. President Roosevelt had won an unprecedented third term in office. Until then, following the precedent set by George Washington, no president had stood for a third time. The 22nd amendment to the United States Constitution limiting a president to two terms would not be ratified until 1951. Roosevelt had

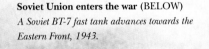

Soviet Union enters the war (BELOW)
A Soviet BT-7 fast tank advances towards the Eastern Front, 1943.

Pushing onwards (ABOVE)
Heavy artillery and crew move to the front line, Libya, 1941.

War extends further (BELOW)
Germans troops join Italian forces in North Africa, 1941.

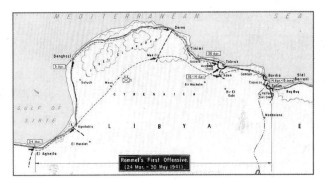

Pearl Harbor (ABOVE)
Smoke rises from Hickam Air Force Base as Japanese planes continue their attack, Pearl Harbor, USA, 1941.

long been seen as a friend of Britain, stretching every fiber to alleviate her plight despite the isolationist sentiment in Congress and the country. Although he and Churchill had only met once before the war and Roosevelt's aides dismissed Churchill as a drunk, Churchill had sought to establish a relationship with Roosevelt through regular telegrams and telephone calls from the time he returned to power as First Lord of the Admiralty in 1939. Churchill's strategy from the beginning was to bring the United States into the war. He saw scant prospects for victory without her.

"UNCLE JOE"

But first Churchill would find himself allied with Stalin. Churchill had always been a staunch anti-Bolshevik and had been behind the Allied intervention into the USSR in 1919, in an attempt to strangle the Soviet State at birth. After Germany attacked the Soviet Union, Churchill was quick to divert much-needed aid to his new-found Soviet ally. A propaganda campaign portrayed the once-feared "man of steel"—Stalin— as the avuncular "Uncle Joe."

Churchill was unapologetic about defending the Soviet dictator in public, saying: "If Hitler invaded hell I would make at least one favorable reference to the devil in the House of Commons." Then, to Churchill's great relief, Japan attacked Pearl Harbor, thereby bringing the US into the war.

War in North Africa

"Ahead of us lay territories containing an enormous wealth of raw materials—Africa, for example, and the Middle East—which could have freed us of all our worries."

Erwin Rommel

With men and materiel diverted to Greece, the British were not able to push home their advantage against the Italians in North Africa. Once again Hitler stepped in and the British found themselves facing a far more formidable foe—fresh from their victory in France, the seasoned Panzer crews of Erwin Rommel, which became known as the Afrika Korps.

ROMMEL ARRIVES IN NORTH AFRICA

The Afrika Korps that Hitler sent "to render services to our allies in the defense of Tripolitania—particularly against the British armored division" was never meant to be more than two divisions. The Panzers were needed for the attack on the Soviet Union that Hitler was planning that summer. On February 12, Rommel arrived in Tripoli. The following day there was a parade of Panzers in the main street. Then they rumbled out of Tripoli, bound for the front. On March 31, Rommel attacked at Agheila, even though his Panzers were not yet up to strength. The Royal Navy still controlled the Mediterranean so he could not expect any reinforcements, but he did not want to give the British time to prepare defenses.

THE DESERT FOX

Although an infantryman by training, Rommel used his Panzers like cavalry, asking his tank crews to make quick changes of directions, feints and sudden withdrawals, which earned him his nickname, the "Desert Fox." As the British put up little resistance, Rommel decided to seize the whole of Cyrenaica (the eastern coastal region of Libya) in one stroke. Speed was now everything. The advance was so rapid that Rommel had to take to the air with the Luftwaffe to keep up with the action. This took the Italians by surprise, who opened fire on German planes. "It was a miracle we were not shot down," wrote Rommel, "and it did not speak well of Italian marksmanship." The advancing Panzers captured General Sir Richard O'Connor, recently knighted for his success against

the Italians, and the whole of his staff. In the desert, Rommel found some discarded British sun-and-sand goggles. Worn over the gold-braided rim of the peak of his cap, these became his trademark. By April 10, the British had retreated all the way back into Egypt, leaving one enclave that would become a symbol of defiance—Tobruk.

DESERT RATS IN TOBRUK

At Tobruk in 1941, German armored formations for the first time were stopped in their tracks by a small force of defiant "Desert Rats." They showed that the Blitzkrieg could be defeated by minefields, artillery, anti-aircraft fire, and infantry who stood their ground in what turned out to be the longest siege in British imperial history.

The Italian fort at Tobruk had fallen effortlessly to the British on January 21, 1941, and its fortifications were largely intact. Its strongpoints were protected by three-foot-thick concrete which offered protection against 15cm guns, the heaviest the German Afrika Korps had at the time. The fort had an anti-tank ditch, camouflaged with planks and sand, and the perimeter defenses were 28 miles long. Field Marshal Erwin Rommel reached Tobruk in April and sent a motorized detachment to storm the town, but it was repulsed by heavy gunfire which killed its commander. Three nights later, the Germans were repulsed again. Meanwhile, elements of the Afrika Korps had bypassed Tobruk and had reached the Egyptian border. From then on, the 22,000 men at Tobruk—largely Australian and Indian—would have to be supplied by sea. However, while the Luftwaffe had complete air superiority, Allied anti-aircraft gunners managed to keep the harbor open.

Assault on Tobruk (RIGHT)
German tanks recapture Italian fort at Tobruk, Libya, despite heavy resistance, 1941.

"DESERT RATS"

Over the next two months, Panzers made repeated attacks on Tobruk that were fended off. By then the Germans had lost 1,700 men, compared to the garrison's casualties of 797—59 killed, 355 wounded, and 383 missing. However, the German High Command grew alarmed at the losses and ordered Rommel not to attack again. Ignoring Rommel's difficulties, Lord Haw-Haw crowed that the garrison was "caught like rats in a trap." A German newspaper then dubbed the British defenders the "Rats of Tobruk," a name they embraced. Rommel now laid siege and repulsed three attempts to break through. Eventually the Axis forces were forced back and the garrison relieved. The Siege of Tobruk lasted 242 days, from April 10 to December 7, 1941, 55 days longer than the siege of Mafeking in the Boer War. It was the first defeat of German land forces in World War II. As well as providing a vital psychological boost, the defense of Tobruk also kept Turkey—Germany's ally in World War I—out of the war. This prevented Hitler from using Turkey as a southern springboard for his attack on the Soviet Union and delayed it by at least a month. As winter is considered to be "Russia's greatest general," this proved crucial.

THE SIEGE OF TOBRUK

"A Stuka was about 50 feet above me and 100 yards or so ahead. It was coming straight at me, guns blazing. Finding an old trench three parts full of sand, with old sandbags, threadbare and torn, around the rim, I threw myself down behind one of the bags at the same time as I felt a thud near my head the other side of the sandbag … After the Stuka had crossed the horizon, I went round the other side of the trench. There I opened my knife and dug a copper-plated bullet out of the sandbag. That bullet I kept for ages, and when we were able to get leave in Cairo, I gave it to an American seaman whom I met in a bar."

Richard Hill, veteran of the siege of Tobruk

North African campaign

Every soldier must know, before he goes into battle, how the little battle he is to fight fits into the larger picture ..."

Field Marshall Bernard Law Montgomery, Commander of the British Eighth Army

The featureless desert of North Africa was the perfect terrain for tank warfare. In 1941, Germany sent a Panzer force—the Afrika Korps—under General Erwin Rommel, who had proved his mastery of the new armored warfare in France the previous year. Out of respect, the British called him the "Desert Fox." But in 1942, when all seemed lost, Churchill gave the command of the British Eighth Army to Bernard Law Montgomery, a military leader who proved himself Rommel's superior. By then, the US had entered the war. While the British pushed Rommel out of Libya, American troops landed to Rommel's rear in Algeria and Morocco. In a matter of months, Rommel's seemingly invincible Afrika Korps had been forced out of North Africa.

Artillery attack (ABOVE)
Soldiers scramble to reload a 25-pound gun while under fire in El Alamein, Egypt, 1942.

Under fire (BELOW)
A German tank squadron comes under heavy fire from British artillery, 1940.

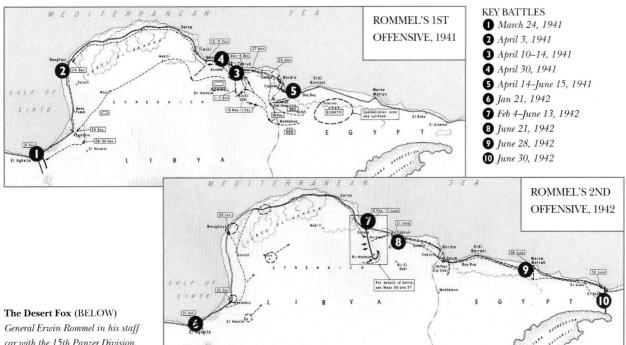

ROMMEL'S 1ST
OFFENSIVE, 1941

ROMMEL'S 2ND
OFFENSIVE, 1942

KEY BATTLES
❶ *March 24, 1941*
❷ *April 3, 1941*
❸ *April 10–14, 1941*
❹ *April 30, 1941*
❺ *April 14–June 15, 1941*
❻ *Jan 21, 1942*
❼ *Feb 4–June 13, 1942*
❽ *June 21, 1942*
❾ *June 28, 1942*
❿ *June 30, 1942*

The Desert Fox (BELOW)
*General Erwin Rommel in his staff
car with the 15th Panzer Division,
somehwere between Tobruk and Sidi
Omar, Libya, 1941.*

Night raid (BELOW)
An anti-aircraft battery opens fire, Tripoli, North Africa, 1943.

Hess flies to Scotland

"Hess did not fly in my name."

Adolf Hitler

On May 10, 1940, Hitler's trusted deputy Rudolf Hess secretly flew alone from Augsburg to Scotland with peace proposals. The British government took no notice. Hess was taken to the Tower of London where he was held as a prisoner of war. Hitler dismissed his mission, saying Hess was suffering from "pacifist delusions."

It remains one of the great mysteries of World War II. How could Rudolf Hess take a plane, fly across Germany, occupied Europe, and the North Sea carrying a peace offering without the permission, or at least the connivance, of the Nazi authorities? Hess had joined the infant Nazi Party in 1920. After the abortive putsch in 1923, he fled to Austria, but returned voluntarily to be imprisoned in Landsberg prison, where he took down and edited *Mein Kampf* from Hitler's dictation. Unswervingly loyal to the Führer, he rose to become his deputy. Over Scotland in May 1940, Hess abandoned his Messerschmitt 110 to crash while he parachuted to the ground. He broke his ankle on landing and was found in a field by a local plowman, who took him home and offered him a cup of tea. Hess said he never drank tea late at night. He asked to be taken to the Duke of Hamilton, a Scottish nobleman and aviator whom he had once met in Berlin.

NO NEGOTIATIONS WITH THE NAZIS

The peace proposal that Hess carried simply reiterated Germany's demand for a free hand in Europe and the restoration of Germany's former colonies. In return, Germany would respect the integrity of the British Empire. The British rejected the peace proposals out of hand, saying that there could be no negotiations with the Nazis. The following day, a German radio station said that Hess was suffering from "hallucinations." Following the war in 1945, he was convicted at Nuremberg of war crimes and sentenced to life imprisonment. Some believe that, at Hitler's behest, Hess had been trying to contact a fledgling peace party, possibly led by King George VI, who had been opposed to Churchill becoming prime minister. From 1966, Hess was the sole inmate of Spandau prison in Berlin, where he was found dead in 1987. The official verdict was suicide by hanging, though there are doubts that a 93-year-old man could have had the strength to hang himself. After Hess's death, Spandau prison was demolished.

HESS EXPLAINS WHY HE CAME

"My coming to England in this way is, as I realize, so unusual that nobody will easily understand it. I was confronted by a very hard decision. I do not think I could have arrived at my final choice unless I had continually kept before my eyes the vision of an endless line of children's coffins with weeping mothers behind them, both English and German, and another line of coffins of mothers with mourning children."

Rudolf Hess, June 10, 1941

Flight for freedom (LEFT)
British officers pose with the wreckage of the Messerschmitt 110 that Hess flew, Scotland, 1941.

Hitler's right hand (INSET)
Rudolf Hess, Hitler's deputy Führer and the second highest ranking member of the Nazi party.

The fall of Crete

"It takes the Navy three years to build a ship. It would take three hundred years to rebuild a tradition."

Admiral Andrew Cunningham, Commander-in-Chief, Mediterranean Fleet

By May 11, 1941, the whole of Greece and its Aegean islands were in German hands—with the exception of Crete. For the British, Crete was a vital toehold in the eastern Mediterranean. Just 500 miles from Alexandria and 200 miles from Tobruk, Allied forces there would be in great danger if the Germans took the airfields on Crete.

The Germans needed Crete as well, not just to starve out Tobruk. From the airbases on Crete, the RAF was still in striking distance of the Romanian oilfields. With Hitler's imminent attack on the Soviet Union about to deprive Germany of USSR oil, he could not afford to be without a supply from Romania. A German plan was drawn up to attack the island using an airborne division and three infantry regiments which would be landed by a hastily requisitioned flotilla. Defending the island were 41,500 men, 10,300 of whom were Greek. There were 17,000 British troops and a large ANZAC (Australian and New Zealand Army Corps) force, comprising 7,700 New Zealanders and 6,500 Australians, who had escaped from mainland Greece. There were few anti-aircraft guns and, after incessant bombing of the airfield, the RAF withdrew its remaining planes to Egypt.

AIRBORNE ASSAULT

The Battle of Crete began on May 20. The Germans had an air fleet of 500 transport planes and 72 gliders, supported by 500 bombers and fighters. At 07:15 hours the gliders landed near Maleme airfield. Then the paratroop drop began. Although the Germans managed to spike some anti-aircraft guns, they secured few of their objectives and were pinned down. But the following morning, a New Zealand commander, mistakenly thinking his forward positions were overrun, ordered a withdrawal from a vital hill, which the Germans immediately took. With airdropped reinforcements, they captured the airfield and began flying in men and ammunition. This was the only battle in the war fought and won entirely by airborne troops.

FURTHER LANDINGS

The Royal Navy caught the first flotilla of German seaborne troops and sank it. But before they could sink the second flotilla, German Stukas attacked, sinking two cruisers and four destroyers. Once German troops were ashore the Luftwaffe prevented any British counterattack. Unable to prevent further landings, the British commander-in-chief Admiral Cunningham ordered an evacuation—despite the danger to his ships—taking over 15,000 men to safety in Alexandria. Another 12,000 were taken prisoner. But eight days' fighting on Crete had cost the Germans more than the entire Balkan campaign. After Crete, Hitler forbade any further use of paratroops, and plans to invade Cyprus and Malta were abandoned.

Captured in Crete (LEFT)
Greek and British POWs intermingle after being captured during the invasion of Crete, 1941.

"*Crete was not yet in our hands but we had to get these ships south of the little island of Gavhos that lies to the south of Crete. There we saw them and were astonished to see that they weren't putting up any anti-aircraft fire. Later I learned that they were out of ammunition. It was easy as there were no fighters … I hit these two ships, the* Kelly *and the* Kashmir. *One was capsizing after we made our turn and was keel up, and the other one was breaking in two and sinking slowly. Oil had flowed out and was burning, and we were seeing many heads swimming in the water and also in the place where the fire was. Our commander started to throw out his life jacket. Many of our crew did the same, throwing down their life jackets to the British who were swimming there.*"

Heinz-Georg Migeed, Luftwaffe pilot, Crete

Invasion of Crete (LEFT)
German paratroopers advance during the invasion of Crete, 1941.

Sinking the *Bismarck*

"The *Bismarck* had put up a most gallant fight against impossible odds worthy of the old days of the Imperial German Navy, and she went down with her colors flying."

Admiral John Tovey, Commander-in-Chief, British Home Fleet

A SURVIVOR'S STORY

"When the skipper gave the order to abandon the ship, we looked for an exit. I was looking around and saw men sitting on a bench and I asked: 'Don't you want to save yourselves?' They said: 'There is no ship coming, the water is too cold, the waves too high, we are going down with the ship.' … When I came out I couldn't believe it. The British were still shooting, and we looked for cover behind one of the six-inch turrets. Bodies were piled around the turrets, they were all dead. The whole deck was full of blood and body parts … Now the ship started turning over. I thought this would be the end. I was only 23 years old, starting living, I was engaged, and there was no chance to save myself. You just have to jump into the water and swim as long as you can. That's what I did …"

Maschinenobergefreiter *Bruno Rzonca, survivor from the* Bismarck

The Nazis claimed that the *Bismarck* was unsinkable. Completed at the end of 1940, the battleship spent fewer than ten days on the high seas before she was hunted down by the Royal Navy and sunk. Hitler's surface fleet never dared go to sea again, leaving only the U-boats to deny the Allies complete mastery of the Atlantic.

On May 18, 1941, Germany's newest and biggest battleship, the 52,600-ton *Bismarck*, accompanied by heavy cruiser *Prinz Eugen*, left their home port in the Baltic on a mission to disrupt Allied shipping in the Atlantic. The entire British Home Fleet was sent to intercept them. They were located in the Denmark Strait between Iceland and Greenland, where the battleship *Prince of Wales* and the battlecruiser HMS *Hood* engaged them. A German shell hit the *Hood*'s magazine. She exploded and sank in two minutes with the loss of 1,416 men: only three

Last stand (RIGHT)
The Bismarck *fires a thunderous volley from her main batteries, shortly before being sunk by the British Navy, 1941.*

survived. The *Bismarck* then escaped into the open sea, but one
of her fuel tanks had been ruptured. While the *Prinz Eugen*
turned for home, the *Bismarck* made for Brest, a naval base in
northwestern France.

CRIPPLED STEERING GEAR

Thirty hours later, the *Bismarck* was sighted by British aircraft in the
Atlantic around 300 miles off the west coast of Ireland. A torpedo-
strike launched from the *Ark Royal* crippled her steering gear and
at 08:27 hours on May 27 the battleships HMS *King George V* and
Rodney closed in for the kill. Their heavy fire silenced the *Bismarck*
within half an hour. By 10:15 hours she was so low in the water that
their shells were passing through the unarmored superstructure
without causing any major damage. At 10:36 hours, the *Bismarck*
rolled over and sank with her flag still flying. British ships rescued
110 German seamen, but they were scared off by a U-boat and left
other survivors in the water. Of the 2,065 crew of the *Bismarck*,
1,995 lost their lives. The *Bismarck*'s sister ship *Tirpitz* spent the rest
of the war in port or hidden in a fjord in Norway, though her
presence was always a threat.

Men overboard (RIGHT)
German sailors are rescued by the crew of HMS Dorsetshire
after the sinking of the Bismarck, *1941.*

Soviet Union invaded

"We have only to kick in the door and the whole rotten structure will come crashing down."

Adolf Hitler

The Molotov–Ribbentrop Pact had been a sham. In *Mein Kampf*, Hitler had made it clear that the destruction of Communism was one of his primary goals. He also wanted USSR territory as far as the Volga River to provide *Lebensraum*—"living space"—for the German people. He considered the Slavs who lived there to be subhuman. They would provide slave labor for his Reich.

In February 1941, British intelligence learned that Germany planned to invade the USSR that spring. The US picked up similar information. Both countries informed Moscow. But Stalin refused to listen, believing that the Non-Aggression Pact was now "cemented in blood." Then at 05:30 hours on June 22, 1941, the German ambassador in Moscow went to see Molotov. He delivered a declaration of war. The reason—or excuse—was "gross and repeated violations" of the Molotov–Ribbentrop Pact. A huge German army was already pouring across a 1,900-mile front from the Baltic to the Black Sea. Stalin believed his information that the Axis forces massing on the USSR's borders were merely there for military maneuvers; therefore the Germans achieved total surprise.

OPERATION BARBAROSSA

In Operation Barbarossa, named after the twelfth-century German founder of the First Reich, Hitler threw some 180 divisions into the Soviet Union—more than 3 million German troops, supported by 30 Romanian and Finnish divisions. There were 19 Panzer divisions with 3,000 tanks; 2,500 aircraft were involved along with 7,000 artillery pieces. The plan was to

Operation Barbarossa (LEFT)
German troops advance through the Soviet Union, and close on Moscow as Red Army troops fall back, 1941.

destroy all Soviet resistance in lightning advances on Leningrad (St. Petersburg), Moscow, and Kiev. When told of the invasion, Stalin had a "nervous collapse" and did not speak for 11 days. But the Soviet Union was hardly defenseless. Stalin had twice or maybe even three times the number of aircraft and tanks that the Germans had and, while many of the aircraft were obsolete, the Soviet Union heavy tanks were superior to any that the Germans deployed against them. Hitler also underestimated Stalin's reserves. There were 150 divisions in the western USSR and Hitler thought the Soviets could call up 50 more. In fact, they brought up another 200 by mid-August. While huge numbers of Soviet soldiers were encircled and taken prisoner, there were always more to block German progress. Hitler also believed that his invasion would cause the Soviet regime to collapse. He was wrong.

Scorched earth (BELOW)
German Panzers pass through the smoking ruin of a USSR town, torched by the former occupants, 1941.

GERMAN ARMY INVADES THE USSR

"Before the offensive started I had been asked how long we thought it would take us to reach Dvinsk [Dünaburg], assuming that it was possible to do so. My answer had been that, if it could not be done inside four days, we could hardly count on capturing the crossings intact. And now, exactly four days and five hours after H-hour, we had actually completed, as the crow flies, a non-stop dash through 200 miles of enemy territory."

Field Marshal Erich von Manstein, commander of the 11th Army

The Atlantic Charter

"Good to have you aboard, Mr. Churchill."

President Roosevelt, August 9, 1941, USS Augusta, *Placentia Bay, Canada*

Following Germany's attack on the Soviet Union, Churchill formed an uneasy alliance with Stalin, but his strategy was still to get the US into the war. President Roosevelt realized that sooner or later America had to join the fray and in August 1941 he and Churchill met at sea to set out a declaration of their war aims, known as the Atlantic Charter.

The British public knew nothing of Churchill's absence when, in early August, he headed out of Scapa Flow—in the Orkney Islands off the north coast of Scotland—into the Atlantic on board the HMS *Prince of Wales*, which made a zigzag route to avoid U-boats. On the voyage, Churchill took the opportunity to relax—watching movies, reading novels, losing at backgammon to Roosevelt's emissary Harry Hopkins, and drinking champagne and brandy. President Roosevelt himself was purported to be on a fishing trip in New England. Instead he was waiting on the USS *Augusta* in Placentia Bay off Newfoundland, Canada, as the HMS *Prince of Wales* sailed in on August 9. When Churchill boarded the USS *Augusta* to meet Roosevelt, he said: "At long last, Mr. President."

DECODERS

Over the next three days, the two leaders discussed the progress of the war. As well as drawing up the Atlantic Charter, Churchill agreed to hand over three ultra-secret "Magic" decoders which broke the Japanese codes. The US used these to eavesdrop on the communications traffic between Tokyo and the Japanese Embassy in Washington, who were still negotiating with the US State Department while the mission to attack Pearl Harbor was underway. However, there was no mention of the attack in these communications, and because the Americans were not yet on a war footing they did not have the manpower to decode and distribute intercepts fast enough. The signing of the Charter was announced on August 14, when both leaders were safely home. In London on September 24, 1941, representatives of Belgium, Czechoslovakia, Greece, Luxembourg, the Netherlands, Norway, Poland, the Soviet Union, Yugoslavia, and the Free French signed the Charter. In all, 26 nations signed what became the basis of the charter of the United Nations.

The big two
President Roosevelt and Prime Minister Churchill meet aboard the HMS Prince of Wales *in Placentia Bay, Canada, 1941.*

THE ATLANTIC CHARTER

The President of the United States of America and the Prime Minister, Mr. Churchill, representing His Majesty's Government in the United Kingdom, being met together, deem it right to make known certain common principles in the national policies of their respective countries on which they base their hopes for a better future for the world.

First, their countries seek no aggrandizement, territorial or other;

Second, they desire to see no territorial changes that do not accord with the freely expressed wishes of the peoples concerned;

Third, they respect the right of all peoples to choose the form of government under which they will live; and they wish to see sovereign rights and self government restored to those who have been forcibly deprived of them;

Fourth, they will endeavor, with due respect for their existing obligations, to further the enjoyment by all States, great or small, victor or vanquished, of access, on equal terms, to the trade and to the raw materials of the world which are needed for their economic prosperity;

Fifth, they desire to bring about the fullest collaboration between all nations in the economic field with the object of securing, for all, improved labor standards, economic advancement and social security;

Sixth, after the final destruction of the Nazi tyranny, they hope to see established a peace which will afford to all nations the means of dwelling in safety within their own boundaries, and which will afford assurance that all the men in all the lands may live out their lives in freedom from fear and want;

Seventh, such a peace should enable all men to traverse the high seas and oceans without hindrance;

Eighth, they believe that all of the nations of the world, for realistic as well as spiritual reasons, must come to the abandonment of the use of force. Since no future peace can be maintained if land, sea or air armaments continue to be employed by nations which threaten, or may threaten, aggression outside of their frontiers, they believe, pending the establishment of a wider and permanent system of general security, that the disarmament of such nations is essential. They will likewise aid and encourage all other practicable measures which will lighten for peace-loving peoples the crushing burden of armaments.

Signed by: Franklin D. Roosevelt & Winston S. Churchill

War in Iraq and Iran

"The Iraqis who were trying to occupy Habbaniya were held off by a very spirited defense by the RAF so they couldn't enter. The moment we came within sight of them, they gave up."

Lieutenant Arthur Wellesley

Since the success of the Blitzkrieg, warfare had become more mechanized, so oil was a vital resource in which the Axis powers were short of supplies. The Middle East, therefore, became key. The British had invaded Iraq (Mesopotamia) during World War I and now did so again. Then, with the Russians, they opened a new southerly supply line through Iran (Persia).

In 1939, Iraq was obliged under its treaties with the British to break off relations with Nazi Germany. However, the Axis powers began stirring up anti-British feeling among Arab nationalists. The prime minister of Iraq, Rashid Ali, fell under the influence of pan-Arabist army officers who began secret negotiations with the Axis powers. In April 1941, the British sent troops into Iraq, claiming that they were saving the country from a coup. After hostilities that lasted just 30 days, Rashid Ali and other pro-German leaders fled, and the British installed Emir Abdullah as prime minister. A new agreement gave Britain access to all road and rail communications in the country. In return, Britain guaranteed to preserve Iraqi independence.

IRAN

On August 25, British and Soviet troops marched into Iran on the pretext that they were dislodging a Nazi "fifth column" of troops who were planning a coup. British and Gurkha troops crossed the border from Iraq, while Indian troops took the port of Bandar Shapur, seizing seven Axis merchant ships. Allied

Refinery guards (ABOVE)
Indian troops march into an oil refinery to act as guards, 1941.

IRAQ SURRENDERS

"If those infernal guns were still there I thought we would soon know. We walked 25 yards, 50 yards ... when we had gone nearly 100 yards I was beginning to think we had got away with it. It came as almost a surprise when a storm of machine-gun fire descended on us. We tried to wriggle into the sand and waited for the terrible cacophony to stop. Luckily they'd opened fire just a shade too soon ... but the Iraqis gave up as soon as their defenses were hit by British 25-pounder guns fired by a second column arriving from the south. They sued for peace and we started having Iraqis coming in, surrendering. They surrendered in droves."

*Lieutenant Arthur Wellesley,
Household Cavalry*

airborne troops took the oilfields, ostensibly to prevent sabotage and protect British workers there. Although there were reports of "bursts of gunfire," it was said that the Iranians largely stood by with an attitude of "benevolent interest." The Red Army invaded from the north between the Caspian Sea and the Turkish border. The invasion secured oil supplies for the Allies and opened a vital supply route for material being sent to the USSR.

Armored column (BELOW)
Armored cars streak across the sands away from Fort Rutbah after its successful capture, 1941.

Supplies en route (below)
*A huge convoy of ships, seen from a patroling US Navy
flying boat, 1941.*

The Arctic convoys

"I am fully aware of the difficulties involved and of the sacrifices made by Great Britain in the matter [the Arctic convoys]. I feel, however, it is incumbent upon me to approach you with the request to take all possible measures in order to ensure the arrival of the above-mentioned materials in the USSR."

Joseph Stalin, message to Winston Churchill, May 1942

Once the Soviet Union had entered the war against Germany, she had to receive supplies from the Allies. Between August 1941 and May 1945, 78 convoys, comprising some 1,400 merchant ships, sailed from Britain and the US to the northern ports of Murmansk and Archangel, delivering vital supplies under the lend-lease program. Eighty-five merchant vessels and 16 Royal Navy escorts were lost in combat.

The Arctic convoys suffered particularly harsh conditions. In winter, the weather was atrocious; in summer, due to the uninterrupted daylight, convoys had to run the gauntlet of German planes, ships, and U-boats based in occupied Norway, and were often suspended. Some doubted that the convoys could get through at all. But the first one, which sailed on August 21, 1941, arrived unscathed in Archangel ten days later. The Polish war artist Felix Topolski and two journalists were used to maximize the event's usefulness as propaganda. There were five convoys in all in 1941, and only one merchant vessel was lost to U-boats. Their losses began to mount in 1942, but the Soviet Union's need for supplies also increased and when Convoy PQ16 assembled off Iceland in May 1942, Churchill declared that even if only 50 percent of all convoys got through, it would be considered worthwhile.

SEA BATTLES

In December 1942 each side lost one destroyer in the Battle of the Barents Sea, but all 14 of the Allied merchant ships got through. In the Battle of the North Cape the following December, the Kriegsmarine lost the battlecruiser *Scharnhorst*, demonstrating to the German Admiral Dönitz that surface ships were no longer effective without radar. Despite the loss of just under 3,000 British sailors, the convoys played a vital role in helping the city of Leningrad—now St. Petersburg— survive its almost 900-day siege from September 8, 1941 to January 27, 1944. After the siege was lifted and the Germans were in retreat, the convoys no longer played such a significant role, though they continued due to their symbolic and strategic value.

LIFE ON AN ARCTIC SHIP

"The Arctic winter lasts for many months and it was often that we went into Russia in the dark and came back in the dark, and it was a bit frightening and a rather unusual life that we spent so many hours in the dark. We had so little time to think about light and darkness and so on because the weather was so disastrous that we were battered around on duty to such an extent that when we were off duty we immediately got our head down and if possible fell asleep, because this was the only thing that kept us going so to be honest the day passed in that way."

Donald Harman, sailor on board HMS Savage, 1941–42

Code-breaking

"In the case of the Enigma, the first solutions were made by hand
by mathematicians relying on German operators' errors."

Harry Hinsley, assistant at Bletchley Park

The Allies' ability to break German and Japanese codes during World War II was of critical importance—so much so that operations and lives were sacrificed rather than alert the enemy to the fact that their codes had been broken. Thousands of people worked on code-breaking, most notably at Bletchley Park in Buckinghamshire, England.

At the end of World War I the Germans had developed a cipher machine called Enigma that they thought could produce an unbreakable code. However, in the 1930s, Polish cryptologists cracked the code and, in 1939, passed their expertise onto the British who set up a top-secret code-breaking group under the gifted mathematician Alan Turing at the country house of Bletchley Park, 50 miles north of London. At the height of the war, thousands of radio intercepts a day were passing through Bletchley Park, including messages from Hitler himself. The resulting intelligence, known as Ultra, was circulated to only a restricted circle of Allied commanders. Later in the war, other German codes had to be broken. To do that the first programmable computer, called Colossus, was developed at Bletchley Park. The British won the Battle of Britain and the Battle of the Atlantic largely because they managed to read Luftwaffe and U-boat signals. Reading Hitler's messages to his commanders also led to the destruction of the German forces during the Battle for Normandy following the D-Day landings. Code-breaking also allowed the British to arrest German spies as well as send false intelligence and judge its effect.

PURPLE

The Germans supplied Enigma machines to the Japanese, who developed their own code called Purple. The British broke this too and handed over the "Magic" decoders to the US in time for American code-breakers to decipher the diplomatic traffic between the Japanese Embassy in Washington and Tokyo before Pearl Harbor (December 7, 1941). Although this failed to alert the US to the attack, decrypting Japanese messages played a significant part in US naval victories in the Coral Sea and at Midway in 1941 and 1942. It also allowed American pilots to shoot down the plane carrying Admiral Isoroku Yamamoto, the architect of the Pearl Harbor attack, on April 18, 1943.

The father of computer science (ABOVE RIGHT)
British scientist Alan Turing, who was instrumental in breaking the German Enigma code, and advanced the field of computer science, 1951.

Caught unawares (LEFT)
Two German U-boats, refueling on the surface, are attacked and damaged by a Grumman Avenger Torpedo Bomber, 1940.

OPERATION DOUBLECROSS

"We read all the Enigma signals of the German Abwehr [Military Intelligence] which meant that we captured every spy that arrived in the United Kingdom by having advance knowledge of his arrival. Which meant that we could turn such as we needed and use them to send messages we wanted the Abwehr to receive, and monitor the reception and the reaction of the Abwehr. All that signal intelligence underlay the effective use of what was called the Doublecross Operation for the purposes both of stopping German reception of intelligence—other than false intelligence— and also of creating deception by sending them false intelligence."

Harry Hinsley, assistant at Bletchley Park

Pearl Harbor

"Yesterday, December 7, 1941—a day which will live in infamy—the United States of America was suddenly and deliberately attacked by the naval and air forces of the Empire of Japan."

President Roosevelt, US Congress, December 8, 1941

At 07:53 hours on Sunday December 7, 1941, 181 Japanese warplanes attacked the US Pacific Fleet as it lay at anchor in Pearl Harbor, the great American naval base on Oahu in the Hawaiian Islands. Forty minutes later, a second wave of 170 planes staged a second attack. There had been no formal declaration, but the United States was now at war with the Axis powers.

At 05:50 hours on the morning of December 7, the Japanese aircraft carriers turned into the wind. Japanese pilots assembled on the decks and tied around their heads ceremonial *hachimaki* scarves carrying the Japanese characters meaning "Certain Victory." By 06:20 hours, 49 bombers, 51 dive-bombers, 40 torpedo-planes, and 41 Zero fighters were heading to Oahu, while the second wave was being marshaled on the Japanese flight decks.

At 07:00 hours, the attack force flight leader Commander Fuchida picked up music from an Hawaiian radio station and locked onto it. Five minutes later, two American radar operators spotted a blip, but were told that a flight of B-17s was expected that morning. The Japanese planes stayed above a thick layer of cloud. Below, it was a quiet Sunday morning. Few men were on deck. The ships were moored close together and none was ready to sail. Of the 300 planes based at the airfields on the island, only three were airborne.

"TORA, TORA, TORA"

At 07:53 hours, Fuchida sent the famous radio message *"Tora, Tora, Tora"*—"Tiger, Tiger, Tiger"—which meant the Americans had been taken completely by surprise. Two minutes later, the Pacific Fleet and the surrounding airfields were under full-scale attack. For the next two hours, bombs and torpedoes rained down. Gunners managed to return fire, but were hampered by listing decks and a shortage of ammunition. Meanwhile, Japanese planes bombed and strafed American airfields against virtually no opposition. The battleship USS *Arizona* blew up and was completely destroyed. The *Oklahoma* capsized. The *California*, *Nevada*, and *West Virginia* sank at their moorings. Three other battleships, three cruisers, three destroyers, and several other vessels also suffered damage. Some 169 aircraft were completely destroyed and 150 damaged, mainly on the ground.

The sinking of USS California (RIGHT)
Black smoke pours from the USS California *after the surprise attack by the Japanese, after which the battleship sank at its moorings, 1941.*

Taken by surprise (LEFT)
USS Shaw *explodes during the Japanese raid on Pearl Harbor, December 7, 1941.*

1942–Timeline

Japanese bomb Rangoon

First US troops land in Britain

Singapore falls to the Japanese

MacArthur leaves the Philippines

Terror bombing of German cities begins

Raid on St. Nazaire

Doolittle Raid

Battle of the Coral Sea

Thousand-bomber raid on Cologne

Battle of the Midway

JANUARY   FEBRUARY   MARCH   APRIL   MAY   JUNE

1942

THE TIDE TURNS

THERE WAS MORE BAD NEWS IN 1942. MALAYA, SINGAPORE, AND THE PHILIPPINES FELL TO THE JAPANESE. HITLER APPROVED THE "FINAL SOLUTION"—THE SYSTEMATIC MURDER OF EVERY EUROPEAN JEW. THE NAZIS BEGAN CLEARING THE WARSAW GHETTO, SENDING ITS WRETCHED INHABITANTS TO EXTERMINATION CAMPS. BUT AFTER MANY DEFEATS, THE ALLIES BEGAN TO SCORE SOME NOTABLE VICTORIES THAT WOULD TURN THE TIDE OF THE WAR.

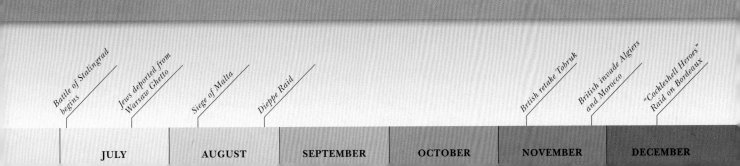

Battle of Stalingrad begins	Jews deported from Warsaw Ghetto	Siege of Malta	Dieppe Raid	British retake Tobruk	British invade Algiers and Morocco	"Cockleshell Heroes" Raid on Bordeaux
JULY	AUGUST	SEPTEMBER	OCTOBER	NOVEMBER	DECEMBER

Although the Russian Red Army had spent six months falling back in retreat, losing millions of men taken prisoner along the way, they had slowed the Germans sufficiently to deny them the Soviet Union's major cities—Moscow, Stalingrad (now Volgograd), and Leningrad (St. Petersburg). The Germans were halted by the Soviet Union's "greatest general"—winter. The Russian people and cities still faced years of suffering, but the Nazi advance in the east had reached its height.

THE WAR IN THE AIR

The British had learnt the lesson of the Blitz and began bombing German cities in earnest. Soon they would be mounting thousands of bomber raids. The first US troops arrived in the UK in 1942. Soon the US Army Air Force—which became the US Air Force in 1947—would follow, launching planes from British airfields to bomb German cities during the day while the British Royal Air Force attacked at night. Meanwhile, the USAAF staged the famous Doolittle Raid. Lieutenant-Colonel James Doolittle led a carrier-launched raid by 16 B-25 bombers on Tokyo and other Japanese cities in a stark warning to the Japanese people of what was to come.

Battle of El Alamein (RIGHT)
Allied tanks chase retreating German troops, Egypt, 1942.

Far East tactics (BELOW)
Torpedoed Japanese destroyer, 1942.

US operations (MAP)
American strategy in the Far East.

ON THE OFFENSIVE

With the aid of American weapons, the British now went on the offensive, making daring commando attacks on the European mainland. Most notable was the raid on Dieppe which, while itself a failure, pointed the way to the D-Day landings in Normandy two years later. In North Africa, the British finally halted Rommel's advance at the gates of Egypt, then, at El Alamein, won the first British victory of the land war. In the following month US troops landed in North Africa, beginning a pincer movement to force the Axis powers out of the continent. In the Far East, too, the British adopted new tactics that eventually held the Japanese back in Burma, while the Australians halted the Japanese advance on the Kokoda Trail in New Guinea. The US took on the Japanese Imperial Navy in the Coral Sea, then, in a decisive battle at Midway, ended Japan's hopes of an empire. After Midway—which happened just six months after the unprovoked attack at Pearl Harbor—Japan would be on the retreat. By the end of 1942, the Axis powers, who had begun the war assured of victory, now began to sample the bitter taste of defeat. Despite the terrible destruction their countries now faced, at no point did they sue for peace.

US Air Force in the UK (LEFT)
American crew celebrate after a successful return.

Germans reach Moscow

"All of a sudden, the men noticed the symptoms of frostbite on each other's faces. The mercury registered minus 35°C."

General Gustav Hoehne, Eastern Front, 1941–42

The Germans had been having all their own way in the USSR. The Red Army was ill-prepared. Its officer corps had been decimated by political purges and Stalin had believed Hitler when he said he would not attack the Soviet Union. But Operation Barbarossa had been delayed by the German intervention in Greece and vital Panzers had been diverted to North Africa.

WINTER CLOTHING AT THE FRONT

"It was possible to requisition some furs and felt boots from the natives for a small fraction of the troops. Winter clothing was also removed from the enemy dead. But it was not until the spring of 1942 that furs, warm underwear, gloves and ear protectors arrived from home, and these too sufficed to supply only a small part of the troops … If a man had a reserve of underwear, he wore two lots. The divisions and army issued the entire supply of underwear they had on hand. Finally, each man succeeded in providing himself with more protection for his head and ears by using pieces of cloth and waistbands. The most difficult problem, for which there was no solution, was that of footwear. Consequently, there were frozen limbs."

Dr. Lother Rendulic, Russian Front

Hitler's Panzers reached Minsk on June 29, 1941, encircling four Soviet armies and taking 287,000 prisoners. On July 16, the Germans surrounded Smolensk, taking a further 300,000 prisoners. At Kiev, they took another 665,000 prisoners, and by October were menacing Leningrad. Another 663,000 prisoners were taken at Vyazma and 100,000 at Bryansk. The road to Moscow was now open. Diplomats were evacuated and the embalmed body of Lenin was removed from his tomb on Red Square for safekeeping. Stalin was about to flee the city, then changed his mind. He recalled Marshal Georgii Zhukov, his ablest general, to command the defense of Moscow.

MUD AND SNOW

In the autumn the weather was changing, with rain turning the roads to mud, slowing the German advance. Dense forest north of Moscow barred the Panzers. Zhukov stationed the last of his tanks to the south and stopped the German advance. The Germans launched one final thrust on Moscow on November 15, and reached the Moscow–Volga canal just 20 miles from the city. Then the weather closed in, hampering the movement of German supplies while the Russian scorched-earth policy denied them support from the land. Hitler had been so confident of a quick victory that he had not even provided his men with winter clothing. That winter was the coldest for 140 years. Soon almost everyone in the German Army was suffering from frostbite. Oil froze in the tanks' engines and firing mechanisms seized up. Hitler blamed his generals. He fired them and took over himself. But there was nothing he could do about the weather. In January 1942, Germans on the Eastern Front came to a halt some 40 miles west of Moscow and the city had been saved.

The Eastern Front (MAP)
The German Army encroaches upon Moscow.

Unprepared for cold (RIGHT)

German soldiers, suffering from the cold and frostbite, are captured on the Eastern Front, USSR, 1942.

EASTERN
FRONT 1942

US troops in Britain

"Your safe arrival here marks a new stage in the World War. It is a gloomy portent for Mr. Hitler; nor will its significance be lost on General Tojo."

Sir Archibald Sinclair, Secretary of State for Air, Dufferin Quay, Belfast, January 26, 1942

On January 26, 1942, some 4,000 US infantry men landed in Northern Ireland. They were the first American troops to set foot on European soil—outside Iceland—since the American Expeditionary Force left after World War I. They were the first of tens of thousands who would be stationed in Britain in the run-up to the Normandy landings.

The first man ashore officially was William H. Henke of Hutchinson, Minnesota. However, Major-General Russell P. Hartle and headquarters staff of the 34th Infantry Division from Fort Dix, New Jersey, had preceded him. At a ceremony in Belfast at 12:15 hours, General Hartle was greeted by the Duke of Abercorn, Governor-General of Ulster, the Prime Minister of Northern Ireland, John W. Andrews, the commander of British troops in Ulster, General G. E. W. Franklyn, and the Secretary of State for Air, Sir Archibald Sinclair who had flown over from London. The arrival of the *Strathaird*, which had sailed from Brooklyn on January 15, was kept secret. Even the band of the Ulster Rifles who were to play the officials ashore were not told where they were going and why. Nevertheless, they managed a credible version of "The Star-Spangled Banner."

US BASES SET UP

Planning for the deployment of US troops in Britain began in April 1941, eight months before America had entered the war and four months before the Atlantic Charter had been signed. The US War Department's plan envisioned the wartime deployment of 87,000 Americans in the UK, around half of whom would be with the USAAF. On May 19, 1941, the US War Department set up a Special Observer Group in Grosvenor Square, London. The following month, US contractors began building US Army bases in Scotland and Northern Ireland. Ten days after Pearl Harbor, they were ready for inspection by the Special Observer Group's quartermaster.

Entering a new stage
*US paratroopers march past a traditional
thatched cottage, England, 1942.*

OBSERVATIONS ON BRITISH CULTURE

"The British are often more reserved in
conduct than we are. So if Britons sit in
trains or buses without striking up
conversation with you, it doesn't mean they
are being haughty and unfriendly. Probably
they are paying more attention to you than
you think. But they don't speak to you
because they don't want to appear intrusive
or rude. ... At first you will probably not like
the almost continual rains and mists and the
absence of snow and crisp cold. Most people
get used to the English climate eventually.
The people ... are not given to back-slapping
and they are shy about showing their
affections. But once they get to like you they
make the best friends in the world. ...The
usual drink is beer, which is not an imitation
of German beer as our beer is, but ale. ...
The British don't know how to make a good
cup of coffee. You don't know how to make a
good cup of tea. It's an even swap. The
British are leisurely—but not really slow.
Almost before you meet the people you will
hear them speaking 'English.' At first you
may not understand what they are talking
about and they may not understand what you
say. The accent will be different from what
you are used to, and many of the words will
be strange. ... British money is in pounds,
shillings and pence. They won't be pleased
to hear you call it 'funny money'."
From Over There: Instructions for American
Servicemen in Britain, 1942

The "Final Solution"

"If the international Jewish financiers in and outside Europe should succeed in plunging the nations once more into a world war, then the result will [be] ... the annihilation of the Jewish race in Europe."

Adolf Hitler, January 30, 1939

Hitler had made no secret of his antipathy toward Jews. From the beginning of his political career he spoke of their "removal" by bloody means. At least half a million Jews had already been murdered by the end of 1941. Then, in January 1942, a meeting was held in Berlin where plans were laid systematically to exterminate all the remaining Jews in Europe.

Although no order has been found showing that Hitler personally authorized the extermination of European Jewry, both Rudolf Hoess, commandant of the extermination camp at Auschwitz, and Adolf Eichmann, who organized the mass murder at all the camps, said such an order existed in the early summer of 1941. Hitler's deputy Hermann Göring, propaganda minister Joseph Goebbels, and the head of the SS Heinrich Himmler also make reference to Hitler ordering the extermination of the Jews.

NUREMBERG LAWS

When Hitler had come to power in 1933, he began passing a series of laws, known as the Nuremberg Laws, which stripped Jews of their rights and citizenship. On the night of November 9, 1938—*Kristallnacht*, or the "Night of Broken Glass"—synagogues and Jewish businesses, homes, schools, hospitals, and cemeteries were vandalized. Ninety-one Jews were killed and the police, rather than arrest the perpetrators, were ordered to arrest the victims. Some 30,000 Jews were detained. In January 1939, Hitler warned that if the world was plunged into another war—which he blamed on the Jews—the result would be "the annihilation of the Jewish race in Europe." When Germany attacked the Soviet Union in 1941, special *Einsatzgruppen* death squads were sent to murder political commissars and Jews. They murdered about 1.2 million, sometimes in systematic mass killings as at Babi Yar, a ravine

outside Kiev where some 100,000 Jews were murdered. But the sheer number of Jews who had fallen into Nazi hands created a problem. By November 1, 1941, the first extermination camps were being built—first Belzec, then Sobibor, Treblinka, Chełmno, and Majdanek, and finally Auschwitz-Birkenau. On January 20, 1940, the Wannsee Conference was convened in Wannsee Villa, Berlin, to discuss the practicalities of mass murder. Leading Nazis there included Eichmann and Himmler's deputy Reinhard Heydrich. The mass execution of Jews began soon after.

Auschwitz arrivals (BELOW)
Jewish internees arrive at the Auschwitz railway terminal, Poland, 1942.

Concentration camp inmates (INSET)
Sachsenhausen internees—the badges on the breast had specific meanings, depending on their shape and color, Germany, 1941.

GOEBBELS ON THE JEWISH QUESTION

"Regarding the Jewish question, the Führer is determined to clear the table. He warned the Jews that if they were to cause another world war, it would lead to their own destruction. Those were not empty words. Now the world war has come. The destruction of the Jews must be its necessary consequence. We cannot be sentimental about it. It is not for us to feel sympathy for the Jews. We should have sympathy rather with our own German people. If the German people have to sacrifice 160,000 victims in yet another campaign in the east, then those responsible for this bloody conflict will have to pay for it with their lives."
Joseph Goebbels, diary entry,
December 13, 1941

War in the Far East

"I said, to the people of the Philippines whence I came, I shall return. Tonight, I repeat those words: I shall return!"

General Douglas MacArthur, speech after arriving in Australia, March 30, 1942

In the months following Pearl Harbor, nothing could stop the Japanese advance. Britain was involved in heavy fighting in North Africa and the defense of its own islands. The US was ill-prepared to defend its possessions in the Pacific—Guam, Wake Island, and the Philippines.

Guam and Wake Island fell to the Japanese the day after the attack on Pearl Harbor. Then on December 10, the Japanese landed in British-held Malaya and on the Philippines. On December 25, the British garrison at Hong Kong surrendered after seven days of fighting in which some 6,000 defenders held off an estimated 40,000 Japanese attackers. The governor-general surrendered when the colony's reservoirs were taken by the Japanese. While Japanese divisions advanced down the Malayan Peninsula against fierce resistance, there were further landings in the Solomon Islands and on New Guinea, threatening Australia. The heaviest blow came when Singapore, a great naval base and fortress considered impregnable, fell to the Japanese on February 15. This left the Allies without a dry dock between Durban, South Africa, and Pearl Harbor, and gave the Japanese Navy a vital base for future operations.

THE PHILIPPINES

General Douglas MacArthur had 160,000 troops, including 19,000 Americans, to defend the Philippines, but the USAAF was caught on the ground. A Japanese bombing raid destroyed the stockpile of torpedoes, rendering US submarines useless. With total air superiority, the Japanese landings on December 10 and 12 were virtually unopposed. On December 26, MacArthur declared the Philippines' capital of Manila open (meaning it would not be fought over) and withdrew to the Bataan Peninsula. On March 11 MacArthur was ordered to leave to carry on the fight from Australia, vowing famously: "I shall return." On April 8, US forces at Bataan surrendered. Between 7,000 and 10,000 men died on the 55-mile "Death March" into captivity. The US garrison at Corregidor surrendered on May 6, leaving the whole of the Philippines in Japanese hands.

The Philippines fall to the Japanese
Japanese troops celebrate after defeating Allied forces to take control of the Philippines, 1942.

JAPAN TO CONQUER THE WORLD

"We will plant the Rising Sun flag, dyed with our life blood, on a far desert with its twinkling stars; when the lion roars beneath the trees. We will drag the very crocodile out of the Ganges, where it flows at the foot of the Himalayas. The paper carp shall flutter high above the City of London. Today Berlin, tomorrow Moscow, and snowy Siberia will be in our hands. Our grandchildren shall raise a monument to us in a Chicago purged of gangsters. And when our time comes to cross the Styx, we will wrestle with the Shades themselves."
Words of the "Bakko Ichiu," the song of the Imperial Japanese Military Academy

Japan advances

"I have offered my life to His Majesty the Emperor. For the sake of the country, I am determined and prepared to lay down my life."

Chief Warrant Officer Sadamur Kamita, 27, the Special Attack Flotilla

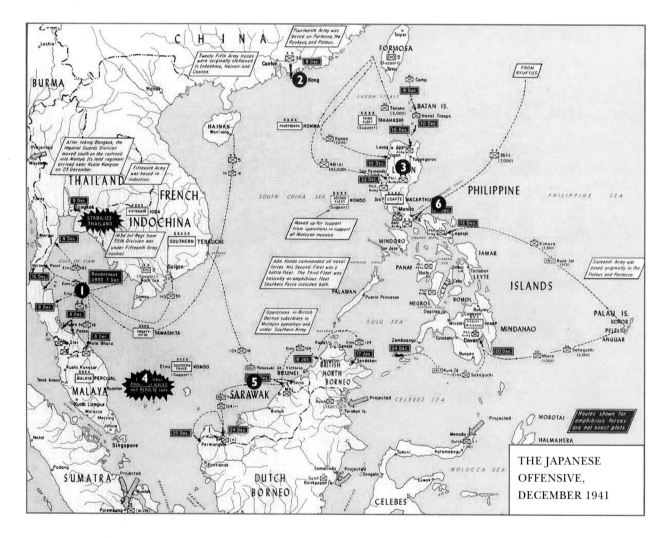

THE JAPANESE OFFENSIVE, DECEMBER 1941

The Japanese strategy was risky. They planned to advance fast enough to secure all the raw materials they needed for their economy, and far enough to keep the enemy at a safe distance from the home islands.

1. Malaya, December 8
2. Hong Kong, December 8
3. Luzon, December 10
4. HMS Prince of Wales *and* HMS Repulse *sunk, December 10*
5. Brunei, 15–16 December
6. Manila, 24 December

Struggling forward (ABOVE)
American soldiers transport their weakened comrades en route to Bataan, the Philippines, 1941.

Japanese victory (ABOVE)
American soldiers surrender to the Japanese, Corregidor, the Philippines, 1942.

Prisoners of war (RIGHT)
Commonwealth POWs in a Japanese camp sort through their meagre clothing rations, 1942.

Before the storm (BELOW)
Japanese crewmen stand to attention, hours before the attack on Pearl Harbor, 1941.

The Home Front

"Our main objective in the OPA is to see to it that American people get the greatest possible protection from rationing and price control—but with the minimum of annoyance."

Lawrence J. Bresnaham, director,
Massachusetts Office of Price Administration, ABC broadcast, October 20, 1943

With industry now dedicated to war production and merchant ships being turned over to military use, the world experienced shortages of food, clothing, and other vital supplies. All countries were affected, and Britain and America introduced a system of rationing.

On January 8, 1940, bacon, butter, and sugar were rationed in Britain, followed by meat, tea, jam, biscuits, breakfast cereals, cheese, eggs, milk, canned fruit, and even soap. However, fish and chips escaped rationing. Ration books were issued to civilians and coupons had to be handed over along with cash when purchases were being made. Generally everyone got the same ration, though children received less and pregnant women more. To supplement their diet, Britons were urged to "Dig for Victory" and grow their own vegetables. In restaurants, the price of a meal and the food on offer was restricted. Gasoline was restricted. Clothing was rationed on a points system. Initially the allowance was for approximately one new outfit per year, but that allowance was progressively cut and people were encouraged to "Make Do and Mend." To save material, hemlines rose. Double-breasted coats, cuffs on pants, buttons on sleeves, and lace and frills on women's underwear disappeared. Women used beetroot as lip rouge, soot for eye shadow, and gravy browning to simulate pantyhose. Razor blades had to be resharpened by running them around a glass and a line was inscribed around baths, even in Buckingham Palace, because no more than five inches of hot water was allowed. Indeed, people were encouraged to have fewer baths, or share a bath. However, many people bought restricted items on the black market.

RATIONING IN THE US

In the US, production of automobiles, household appliances, and houses stopped. Meat, sugar, butter, coffee, gasoline, tires, shoes, and clothing were rationed, but bread, milk, and beer were not. Local schools set up stations where people could get their ration coupons, and teachers handled the paperwork. With half of all canned goods going to the US military or to the Allies, Americans cultivated 20 million "Victory Gardens" to provide vegetables. Although there was no shortage of gasoline, automobile drivers received coupons for just three gallons per week as this was a simple way to reduce tire wear when rubber was in short supply. People eating in restaurants had to pay with cash and ration coupons. The government prosecuted black marketeers, though families and neighbors who illegally sold or traded ration coupons were rarely prosecuted.

Coupon shopping (LEFT)
Children use their ration coupons for basic goods, 1942.

Waiting for rations (BELOW)
Crowds line up to receive sugar rations, 1942.

TYPICAL WEEKLY RATION IN BRITAIN

1s 2d (approximately 1 lb 3 oz) of meat (offal and sausages were not rationed)
4 oz of bacon or ham
3 pints of milk (or 1 packet of milk powder a month)
2 oz butter
2 oz margarine
2 oz fat or lard
2 oz tea
1 egg (or 1 packet of egg powder—making the equivalent of 12 "eggs"—a month)
2 oz jam
3 oz sugar
1 oz cheese
3 oz sweets
2 lb onions
(Plus 16 ration points a month for tinned and dried food.)

The Battle of Stalingrad

"As far as the eye can see, armored vehicles and half-tracks are rolling forward over the steppes. Pennants float in the shimmering afternoon air."

German observer, June 28, 1942

Despite the privations of his men on the Eastern Front, throughout the winter of 1941 Hitler was not downhearted. Most of the Soviet Union's European territory was now in his hands and, by February 1942, the Soviets' winter counterattack had petered out. Now Hitler began to make plans to crush the Red Army once and for all.

The renewed campaign would center on Stalingrad (now Volgograd), a city that stretched some 30 miles along the Volga 600 miles southeast of Moscow. A huge new industrial city, it was paraded as one of the great achievements of the Soviet system. It bore Stalin's name and he realized that the city must be held at all costs. If it fell, so would he. For Hitler, Stalingrad was a symbol of Communism and had to be crushed. It was also a center of armaments production. Once it was taken, his victorious army would encircle Moscow and take the oilfields of the Caucasus. On June 28, on a front stretching from Kursk to Rostov, the German Panzers roared across the steppes. The dust pall they kicked up could be seen for 40 miles and it was soon joined by smoke from burning villages. There was no significant opposition, because Red Army reserves were being held back for the defense of Moscow. But as Germany's finest soldiers massed for the final assault on Stalingrad, Stalin committed the Moscow reserve. Under General Friedrich Paulus, the German Sixth Army made a ferocious attempt to storm Stalingrad before they could arrive. On August 22, German troops penetrated the northern suburbs. The following day, they reached the Volga, within mortar range of a vital railway bridge. The Luftwaffe then delivered an all-out night bombardment. Civilians fled across the Volga, but Stalin stopped the evacuations. Workers in the tractor factories continued producing tanks almost until the Germans were upon them. Then they picked up their weapons to defend their city, while women, children, and the elderly hid in cellars and sewers below.

"NO LAND ACROSS THE VOLGA"

The Germans were the masters of the Blitzkrieg. They were not used to slow, grinding, man-to-man fighting through the rubble of a ruined city. After weeks of ceaseless fighting against crack German troops, the Red Army still held a nine-mile strip along the banks of the Volga. On September 13, Hitler ordered a new offensive. Paulus sent in three Panzer divisions and eight divisions of infantry. Against them, the Soviets had 40 tanks, all but 19 immobile, and three infantry divisions. General Vasili Chuikov inspired his men with the words: "There is no land across the Volga." For those who did not get the message, there were firing squads. Just a few hundred yards from the river, the Germans felt victory was certain and got drunk on looted vodka. But Soviet riflemen and machine gunners hid in ruined buildings, craters, and behind mountains of rubble. The Panzers were vulnerable to grenades dropped from above. House-to-house combat developed, fought with bullet, grenade, bayonet, and flame thrower. Once the Germans thought they had cleared a house, the Russians would retake it, often by knocking through the walls a floor above. Their stout resistance brought the German assault to a halt. For the Germans, two months of fighting for a narrow strip of a ruined city was a propaganda disaster. Meanwhile General Zhukov had been sent for and was building up strength for a counterattack.

Urban warfare
German soldiers entrenched in primitive barricades on the streets of Stalingrad, 1941.

Terror bombing begins

"The ultimate aim of an attack on a town area is to break the morale of the population which occupies it … First, we must make the town physically uninhabitable and, secondly, we must make the people conscious of constant personal danger."

British Air Staff paper, September 23, 1941

The RAF Bomber Command had not done well during the early years of the war. While the Luftwaffe blitzed British cities, the RAF had restricted themselves to the precision bombing of German military and industrial targets. This tactic failed, so in March 1942 they began the terror bombing of German cities.

Analysis of aerial photographs showed that fewer than a third of the bombs dropped by Bomber Command during the first two years of the war were effective. Due to equipment failure, enemy action, weather, or simply getting lost, only about five percent of the planes that set out got within five miles of their target. As a result, there were plans to reallocate the RAF's resources to the army and navy. RAF commanders responded with a report of their own. They analyzed the damage inflicted on British cities by the Blitz and concluded that a bomber force of 4,000 could destroy the 58 German towns with a population of more than 100,000. This should weaken Germany sufficiently to allow British armed forces back in to Continental Europe. On February 14, 1942, the Air Ministry issued the Area Bombing Directive authorizing Bomber Command to attack "without restriction" primary targets that included Essen, Duisburg, Düsseldorf, and Cologne, and secondary targets that included Braunschweig, Lübeck, Rostock, Bremen, Kiel, Hanover, Frankfurt, Mannheim, Stuttgart, and Schweinfurt. Operations were to be focused on the "morale of the enemy civilian population and in particular, the industrial workers." Eight days after the directive was issued, Air Marshal Arthur Harris—known universally as "Bomber" Harris—was appointed head of Bomber Command.

Allied retaliation

German civilians pick their way through heavily damaged streets.

THE EFFECTS OF BOMBING RAIDS

"Careful analysis of the effects of raids on Birmingham, Hull and elsewhere have shown that, on the average, one ton of bombs dropped on a built-up area demolishes 20–40 dwellings and turns 100–200 people out of house and home. We know from our experience that we can count on nearly fourteen operational sorties per bomber produced. The average lift of the bombers we are going to produce over the next fifteen months will be about 3 tons. It follows that each of these bombers will in its life-time drop about 40 tons of bombs. If these are dropped on built-up areas they will make 4000–8000 people homeless. In 1938 over 22 million Germans lived in 58 towns of over 100,000 inhabitants, which, with modern equipment, should be easy to find and hit. Our forecast output of heavy bombers (including Wellingtons) between now and the middle of 1943 is about 10,000. If even half the total load of 10,000 bombers were dropped on the built-up areas of these 58 German towns the great majority of their inhabitants (about one-third of the German population) would be turned out of house and home. Investigation seems to show that having one's home demolished is most damaging to morale. People seem to mind it more than having their friends or even relatives killed. At Hull signs of strain were evident, though only one-tenth of the houses were demolished. On the above figures we should be able to do ten times as much harm to each of the 58 principal German towns. There seems little doubt that this would break the spirit of the people."
The "Dehousing Paper," September 22, 1941

Pacific naval battles

"Five minutes! Who would have dreamed that the tide of battle would shift completely in that brief interval of time?"

Commander Mitsuo Fuchida

In May 1942, the Japanese were still on the offensive. They planned to strengthen their hold over the Solomon Islands and take New Guinea, cutting Australia off from the US and forcing Australia out of the war. Their plan was thwarted by an Allied fleet in the first sea battle to be fought entirely by aircraft.

BATTLE OF THE CORAL SEA

The Japanese assembled two seaborne invasion forces. One landed unopposed on Tulagi, in the southern Solomons. A larger one was heading for Port Moresby. They were protected by a Japanese fleet led by the aircraft carriers *Shoho, Shokaku,* and *Zuikaku*, with their escorting cruisers and destroyers. But the US Navy could read the Japanese codes and sent two of its own aircraft carriers, plus destroyers and cruisers, including two from the Australian Navy. On May 7, 93 US torpedo bombers attacked the Japanese fleet in the Coral Sea between the Solomons and Australia, and sunk the *Shoho*. The following day, another US attack put the *Shokaku* out of action, but Japanese dive-bombers inflicted such damage on the carrier *Lexington* that she was eventually scuttled. The US destroyer *Sims* and the tanker *Neosho* were also sunk, while the *Yorktown* was slightly damaged and ordered to withdraw. Meanwhile the Japanese retreated to Rabaul, towing the stricken *Shokaku*.

Avengers over Norfolk (LEFT)
A squad of TBF Avenger Torpedo Bombers fly in tight formation over Norfolk, England, 1942.

HELL-DIVERS IN THE PACIFIC

"At 10:24 hours the order to start launching came from the bridge by voice-tube. The Air Officer flapped a white flag, and the first Zero fighter gathered speed and whizzed off the deck. At that instant a lookout screamed: 'Hell-divers!' I looked up to see three black enemy planes plummeting toward our ship. Some of our machine guns managed to fire a few frantic bursts at them, but it was too late. The plump silhouettes of the American Dauntless dive-bombers quickly grew larger, and then a number of black objects suddenly floated eerily from their wings. Bombs! Down they came straight toward me! I fell intuitively to the deck and crawled behind a command post."
Flight Commander Mitsuo Fuchida on board the aircraft carrier Akagi

STRATEGIC VICTORY

Tactically the Japanese won the Battle of the Coral Sea: America had lost one full fleet carrier and two other ships, while the Japanese had lost only one light carrier. However, it was a strategic success for the Allies because the Japanese had to cancel their invasion of Port Moresby.

THE BATTLE OF MIDWAY

Admiral Yamamoto had said that after Pearl Harbor he would "run wild" for six months. He was right. Exactly six months later, the US Pacific Fleet won a decisive victory at Midway Island, ending Japan's imperial ambitions. After Midway, Japan would always be on the retreat.

Following the Battle of the Coral Sea, Yamamoto went back on the offensive. He planned to take Midway Island, 1,300 miles northwest of Oahu. From there, he would be able to mount further attacks on Pearl Harbor, denying America any naval base west of San Francisco and preventing another Doolittle Raid. He should have had the advantage. With the *Yorktown* out of action, the US only had two carriers, the *Hornet* and the *Enterprise*, operational in the Pacific. The Japanese had four—the *Kaga, Akagi, Soryu,* and *Hiryu.* "Purple" intercepts informed US Commander-in-Chief of the Pacific Fleet Admiral Chester Nimitz that Yamamoto planned to stage a diversionary attack on the Aleutian Islands, drawing the US Navy off while

Lost at sea (LEFT)
Japanese heavy cruiser Mikuma *sinks after the Battle of Midway, 1942.*

Admiral Nagumo, the victor of Pearl Harbor, attacked on Midway. However, the *Hornet,* the *Enterprise,* and the rapidly refitted *Yorktown* would be waiting for him.

INVASION CANCELLED

Early on June 4, Nagumo sent a strike force of 108 planes to attack Midway Island. A second wave was armed with torpedoes to attack the US fleet, now thought to be in the area. However, attacks from American land-based planes convinced Nagumo that a second strike was needed on Midway. The Japanese planes were having their torpedoes replaced with bombs when American dive-bombers attacked. The *Kaga* was sunk and the *Akagi* and *Soryu* damaged so badly that they had to be abandoned. The *Hiryu* then launched an attack on the *Yorktown,* which was badly damaged. Late in the afternoon, planes from the *Enterprise* attacked the *Hiryu.* She was scuttled the next day. A Japanese heavy cruiser was also sunk. The *Yorktown* was sunk by a Japanese submarine on June 6, but the rump of the Japanese fleet withdrew and the invasion of Midway was canceled.

Thousand-bomber raid

" The Nazis entered this war under the rather childish delusion that they were going to bomb everyone else, and nobody was going to bomb them. At Rotterdam, London, Warsaw, and half a hundred other places, they put their rather naive theory into operation. They sowed the wind, and now they are going to reap the whirlwind."

Air Marshal Arthur "Bomber" Harris

British Air Marshal Arthur "Bomber" Harris felt that Bomber Command had yet to prove its worth, so he planned a bombing raid on a German city that would be so devastating that the German people would force their leaders to sue for peace. For propaganda purposes, he wanted the raid to be carried out by a thousand planes.

It was a daring plan and new tactics had to be devised to minimize the possibility of mid-air collisions. Coastal

Command pulled out at the last moment and Harris had to make up numbers using planes flown by trainee pilots and their instructors. Harris wanted to bomb Hamburg, a vital sea port. Churchill favored Essen, the center of German industry. But the strategists advised that Cologne would be a better target because it was closer and, as a rail hub, its destruction would make it difficult for Germany to move men and equipment around. At 22:30 hours on May 30, 1942, bombers began taking off from 53 air bases across Britain. Once over the Continent, crews were told to look for the Rhine and follow it until they reached Cologne. The planes flew above the clouds over Western Europe, but these cleared over the city which was bathed in the light of a full moon.

INCENDIARY BOMBS LIGHT THE WAY

More than 2,000 tons of bombs were dropped on Cologne—four times the amount dropped on the worst night of the Blitz. Within 15 minutes, the old town was ablaze. The glow of the flames could be seen 100 miles away and smoke rose 15,000 feet in the air. It was so dense that the RAF could not get any usable reconnaissance photos of the city for a week. Six hundred acres of the city had been razed to the ground, 13,000 homes destroyed, another 6,000 badly damaged, and 45,000 people made homeless. Some 469 were killed and there were 5,000 casualties. Of the 1,046 bombers that took part in the raid, 39 were lost—four in mid-air collisions over the target, the

rest mainly to night fighters. Four percent of planes were lost, which was considered the maximum loss that Bomber Command could sustain. However, although Cologne was paralyzed for a week, within six months it had recovered and Germany did not surrender. Indeed, within hours it had mounted a bombing raid of its own on historic Canterbury.

COLOGNE BADLY DAMAGED

"I have talked with comrades who returned from leave in Cologne. They told me that one-third of the city is a pile of rubble and that there is much anguish and misery ... it is no use for us to destroy the Russians, while the English destroy our homes."
Letter from a German soldier to his mother

Air raids on Germany
Stirling bombers in formation leave the UK for a bombing raid across the English Channel.

Malta

> "When we entered Valletta Harbor, we were saluted like a victorious naval ship. Crowds of people were singing and shouting and screaming."
>
> *Merchant Seaman Jan Larsen, 27, SS* Santa Elsa

Lying at the narrow waist of the Mediterranean, Malta was of vital strategic importance. Taken by the British in 1814 after the fall of Napoleon, it now lay astride the Axis supply route from Sicily to North Africa and the British route to Alexandria. Malta received such a pounding in 1942 that its people were awarded the George Cross, Britain's highest civilian decoration for courage.

The British Army and Air Force declared that Malta could not be defended. The Royal Navy disagreed and based submarines there. The island was within easy reach of Axis air fields on Sicily, and British and American aircraft carriers ferried Spitfires and Hurricanes within flying range of Malta to see off the Nazi attackers. It was also difficult to keep the island supplied. Only fast minesweepers could put in there. British submarines were modified to carry gasoline and ammunition, and remained submerged on the harbor seabed during daylight. However, military planners realized that Malta would be forced to surrender if more fuel, grain, and ammunition did not get through before the end of August 1942.

A SHIP'S CHAPLAIN'S ACTION DIARY

In his action diary for August 12, 1942, HMS Rodney's chaplain Kenneth Thompson made 80 entries between 0745 and 2015. At the height of the action, he recorded:
1236 Mine, bomb or torpedo explodes astern
1239 Manchester opens fire
1241 Destroyers open fire port side
1242 Nine torpedo bombers coming in outside screen
1243 16" open fire to port
1245 Torpedoes dropped port bow
12:48 Six torpedo bombers on port beam
1248 Torpedo bomber shot down by fighter red 10

OPERATION PEDESTAL

Fourteen merchant vessels guarded by 64 warships made a desperate attempt to relieve the island in Operation Pedestal. On August 10, 1942, the convoy passed through the Straits of Gibraltar in three groups. Within 24 hours a U-boat slipped around four destroyers to torpedo HMS *Eagle*, one of the three aircraft carriers with the flotilla. She sank in six minutes with the loss of 160 men and a third of the convoy's air defenses. Successive U-boat attacks targeted the SS *Ohio*, the world's then-biggest tanker carrying 107,000 barrels of oil vital to the operation. She was torpedoed on August 12 and hit by two more bombs the next day. Although crippled, she did not sink. HMS *Ledbury* and other warships came alongside, and towed her into port. Six ships and ten merchantmen had been lost, but Malta had been saved. Within months the Axis powers had given up trying to take the island, and Malta became a vital forward base for the invasion of Italy the following year.

Malta is saved (RIGHT)
British cruisers and aircraft carriers escort convoys carrying supplies and reinforcements into Malta.

Supplies to Malta (LEFT)
HMS Fearless, *destroyed while escorting an Allied convoy to Malta.*

Raids on French ports

"Of the many brave and dashing raids carried out by the men of Combined Operations Command, none was more courageous or imaginative …"

Lord Louis Mountbatten

From the very first conference of the Anglo-American allies held in Washington, D.C. on December 31, 1941, the US had committed itself to an invasion of northern France. But the British dragged their feet. After two years of war, they were wary of chancing all on one risky operation. Their worst fears were realized in a disastrous raid on Dieppe in August 1942.

THE DIEPPE RAID

On August 19, 1942, some 1,000 Canadians, 1,000 British, and 50 US Rangers were put ashore at the French port of Dieppe to test the newly developed LCT—landing craft, carrying tanks—and probe the coastal defenses. The aim was to seize and hold a major port for a short period, both to prove it was possible and to gather intelligence from prisoners and captured materiel while assessing the German response. Supported by the Royal Navy and RAF, the raid was also intended to draw the Luftwaffe into a large, preplanned encounter. But its principal purpose was political—to assure the US of the British willingness to wage war.

DISASTER

German air and sea attacks and their rapid reaction on shore made the landing a disaster. Of the 6,100 troops who embarked only 2,500 returned, including 1,000 who never landed. The rest were killed or captured. Little damage was done to the defenses and the air battle was indecisive. Hitler claimed that a full-scale invasion had been repulsed, saying that over 300 invasion barges and 28 tanks had been destroyed, while three destroyers, two motor torpedo boats, and two transports had been sunk. Mountbatten issued a communiqué denying that the exercise had been an invasion, merely a raid. Despite the outcome, Dieppe did nothing to dampen US enthusiasm for an invasion of northern France, though the British insisted there be no attempt to take a port. Other valuable lessons had been learned, which would be put into practice on D-Day.

COCKLESHELL HEROES RAID ON BORDEAUX

The Royal Navy had denied the Germans the use of the English Channel. However, the German forces in France could still be supplied through the Atlantic port of Bordeaux, which also served as a U-boat base. A bombing raid on the port would have led to many French casualties and was ruled out. So on December 7, 1942, a team of British commandos staged a daring raid.

The aim of Operation Frankton was to destroy as many ships in the port as possible, blocking the harbor with wreckage and rendering it unusable. The 12-man team employed derived their nickname "Cockleshell Heroes" from their two-man canoes which were known as "cockleshells." They were only told what their target was once the submarine HMS *Tuna* that conveyed them had surfaced off the French coast. The plan was for the commandos to paddle across five miles of open sea to the mouth of the River Gironde, then paddle another 70 miles up the river and plant limpet mines on the ships in the harbor. After that they were to abandon their canoes and head for home by way of Spain, which had remained neutral.

CAUGHT AND SHOT

The raid started badly when one of the canoes was holed as it was being made ready on the *Tuna*. Then, as the remaining canoes approached the mouth of the Gironde, they hit a rip tide and another canoe was lost along with its crew. Another two crews were caught and shot. The raiders were left with just two canoes. By then, the Germans knew that something was up and had increased their patrols. Hiding by day and paddling by night, the two crews managed to elude them. In the harbor, they placed limpet mines on the merchant ships they found. The mines were armed with an eight-minute fuse, giving the two crews time to get away. They succeeded in sinking one ship and damaging four others, disrupting the use of the harbor for months. Two members of one crew were caught and shot, the other two-man crew made it home. Such was the significance of the raid that Winston Churchill said that it helped to shorten the war by six months.

THE ESCAPE

With the help of the French Resistance, the two survivors, Major "Blondie" Hasler and Marine Bill Sparks reached Spain, then moved on to Gibraltar. But their problems were not over. The Chief of Combined Operations, Lord Louis Mountbatten, had assumed that all members of the raid were dead, so anyone claiming to be them was treated with the utmost suspicion. Hasler used his rank to get transported back to Britain, but Sparks was arrested. Ever resourceful, he managed to give his military police escort the slip at Euston Station and, after visiting his father, reported to Combined Operations Headquarters.

Allied tanks captured
A British tank landing vessel and two British tanks captured by the Germans during the raid on Dieppe.

REPORT OF THE DIEPPE RAID

"For eight hours, under intense Nazi fire from dawn into a sweltering afternoon, I watched Canadian troops fight the blazing, bloody battle of Dieppe. I saw them go through the biggest of the war's raiding operations in wild scenes that crowded helter-skelter one upon another in crazy sequence. There was a furious attack by German E-boats while the Canadians moved in on Dieppe's beaches, landing by dawn's half-light. When the Canadian battalions stormed through the flashing inferno of Nazi defenses, belching guns of huge tanks rolling into the fight, I spent the grimmest twenty minutes of my life with one unit when a rain of German machine-gun fire wounded half the men in our boat and only a miracle saved us from annihilation."
Ross Munro of The Canadian Press, August 19, 1942

The Warsaw Ghetto

"We saw ourselves as a Jewish underground whose fate was a tragic one, the first to fight. For our hour had come without any sign of hope or rescue."

ZOB fighter

As part of Hitler's "Final Solution," Jews in countries under Nazi control were herded into ghettos, where they were confined until they could be transported to death camps. One of the most notorious ghettos was in Warsaw, Poland. In July 1942, Nazi orders were given for it to be cleared.

The old Jewish quarter of Warsaw was enclosed by a brick wall 11 miles long and 10 feet high. Jews from the surrounding region were herded into it until, in the summer of 1942, it had nearly half a million inhabitants. Many had no accommodation. Those that did were packed nine to a room. Thousands died each month from starvation, typhus, and other diseases. Beginning on July 22, 1942, 5,000 Jews a day were transported to the newly established death camp at Treblinka 50 miles away. The terrible fate that awaited them was not immediately clear to those who were left behind, and the ghetto population had dwindled to just 55,000 when the Jewish Fighting Organization—*Zydowska Organizacja Bojowa*—took control. When SS chief Heinrich Himmler visited the ghetto on January 9, 1943, he ordered another 8,000 deportations. This time the deportees did not report as instructed. When German troops entered the ghetto to search for them, they were attacked by members of the ZOB, who escaped over the rooftops.

HITLER'S BIRTHDAY

On April 19—the first day of Passover—Himmler sent in 2,000 SS men and German soldiers, supported by tanks and artillery, who were ordered to liquidate the Polish Jews by the following day, Hitler's birthday. They were attacked by 1,500 Jewish guerrillas armed with antiquated pistols and rifles, one machine gun, and homemade bombs, which destroyed several tanks. The Germans used police dogs, gas, and flame-throwers to root out the remaining Jews, even flooding the sewers where members of the ZOB took refuge. On May 8, the Germans finally located the ZOB headquarters where its leader, 23-year-old Mordecai Anielewicz, and others committed suicide to avoid being captured. The resistance ended on May 16, when the guerrillas ran out of ammunition. The remaining Jews were killed or sent to death camps. SS Major-General Jürgen Stroop then blew up the Great Synagogue of Warsaw, writing in his report: "The Warsaw Ghetto is no more."

LETTER FROM THE ZOB LEADER

"Peace be with you, my dear friend. Who knows whether we shall meet again? My life's dream has now been realized: Jewish self-defense in the ghetto is now an accomplished fact. I have been witness to the magnificent, heroic struggle of the Jewish fighters."
ZOB leader Mordecai Anielewicz, last letter to a friend, April 23, 1943

German troops enter the ghetto
Two Jewish resistance fighters arrested by German troops after the uprising in the Warsaw Ghetto, Poland, 1943.

Women at war

"We can do it!"

Rosie the Riveter

Women played a vital role in World War II. They worked in the munitions factories making weapons, and on farms producing foods. They flew and fought, became nurses and secret agents. In Europe, even those women who remained housewives suffered terrible privations and the dangers of air-raids. In the Soviet Union, women were employed in combat roles as pilots, snipers, machine gunners, tank drivers, partisans, and political officers. In the Far East, tens of thousands of women, mainly from Korea and China, were coerced into sexual slavery in "comfort stations" as prostitutes for Japanese soldiers.

WOMEN IN BRITAIN

In Britain, women made a vital contribution to the "Home Front," coping with rationing, recycling, and doing war work. They were drafted into factories and the Women's Land Army, replacing male farm workers who had been called up. In all, 1,700,000 women between the ages of 20 and 30 were conscripted into war work, releasing men into the military. Then after 1943, all women had to do part-time work for the war effort. They were also recruited into non-combat

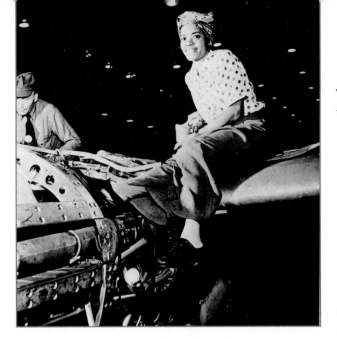

Working through the war (LEFT)
Female riveter in California.

military units such as the Women's Royal Naval Service and the Auxiliary Territorial Service, allowing men to be sent to the front line. The Air Transport Auxiliary also recruited women to deliver planes. British women were not recruited into regular combat units, but the Special Operations Executive used them as agents and radio operators in Nazi-occupied Europe, where they met and worked alongside French and Polish women who were working for the Resistance.

WOMEN IN THE US

By 1945, more than 2.3 million women were working in the war industries in the US, building ships, planes, vehicles, and weaponry, where their role as skilled labor was symbolized by the "Rosie the Riveter" poster. Women also worked on farms and drove trucks, providing logistic support for soldiers. American women first saw combat as army and navy nurses at Pearl Harbor. The Women's Naval Reserve and US Marine Corps Women's Reserve were created for women performing auxiliary roles. They also performed non-combat military service in the Navy WAVES—Women Accepted for Volunteer Emergency Service—and Women's Auxiliary Air Force. In 1943 the Women's Army Corps became officially part of the regular army, but women did not join combat units. Of the 350,000 American women who served in the armed forces, 16 were killed in action, while 67 army and 16 navy nurses spent three years as prisoners of war of the Japanese. Nearly a million women were recruited into the Federal Government for war work.

Wartime harvest (LEFT)
Women gather in the rye harvest in East Suffolk, UK, 1942.

WOMEN IN THE ATS

"I was sixteen when I saw a poster showing a steel-helmeted girl behind a gun. The poster was recruiting for the ATS, for girls to man ack-ack gun sites. I was underage, but you did not have to produce a birth certificate to get in, so I enlisted. The old major who was conducting the swearing in looked me straight in the eyes and said: 'You're not old enough.' And I was out. So I went to the recruitment office in another town, only to come up against the same old major. This time he let me through … The whole battery was sent north to the Sunderland area. All movements were made at night in packed troop trains. We slept in Nissen huts near the gun post. The docks were being bombed night after night. When the alarm sounded the gun post was manned in minutes. The moment the aircraft was spotted, the height finder would shout 'on target' and give the height and range of the plane. The predictor girls would work out the fuse and shout this to the gunners who set the shells. Then all hell was let loose as the four huge guns fired at the same time. During this time, we were credited with bringing down eight enemy aircraft, one of the first mixed batteries to do so. I was one of those in the regiment to receive an honor for this—I was awarded the British Empire Medal."
Sergeant Barbara Bowers

El Alamein

"This is not the end. It is not even the beginning of the end. But it is, perhaps, the end of the beginning."

Winston Churchill, Mansion House, City of London, November 10, 1942

The war had been going on for three years and Britain was yet to win a victory on land against Germany. Then in November Churchill told the House of Commons "we have a new experience. We have victory—a remarkable and definite victory." He ordered the sounding of the church bells that had remained silent since the threat of invasion had been lifted in 1940.

With Britain facing defeat by Field Marshal Rommel in North Africa, Churchill flew to Egypt on August 4 to see what could be done. When General Auchinleck told him that any offensive would have to be delayed until September, Churchill replaced him as commander-in-chief by General Sir Harold Alexander and gave command of the badly demoralized Eighth Army to General Bernard Montgomery. He reorganized the divisions and strengthened the line in the south where he expected Rommel to attack. With the aid of a sandstorm, the British held back the final assault of the Afrika Korps.

FULL RETREAT

Montgomery then abandoned the conventional wisdom of outflanking the enemy's line to the south and, after a 1,000-gun bombardment, began an infantry assault along the coast road on the night of October 23. An armored assault followed. During a week of heavy fighting, losses mounted. Then on November 2, the British punched through the German line ten miles to the south. In the ensuing tank battle, the Germans were decisively defeated. Although Hitler ordered Rommel to hold his ground, Rommel ordered a full retreat on November 5. Montgomery followed cautiously, retaking Tobruk on November 12. There was no need to risk another overturn at the hands of Rommel as US troops had now landed in Morocco and Algeria, some 2,000 miles to his rear. It was a turning point. As Churchill said: "Before Alamein we never had a victory, after Alamein we never had a defeat." The BBC broadcast the sound of the church bells ringing in Britain, so that they could be heard by the people in Occupied Europea—and in Germany itself.

Breakthrough in the desert (BELOW)
British General Bernard L. Montgomery watches Allied tanks advance, North Africa, 1942.

Allied assault (BELOW)
British tanks advance through the desert during the Battle of El Alamein.

LETTER FROM ROMMEL TO HIS WIFE

"Dearest Lu,
The battle is going very heavily against us. We're simply being crushed by the enemy weight. I've made an attempt to salvage part of the army. I wonder if it will succeed. At night I lie open-eyed racking my brains for a way out of this plight for my poor troops. We are facing very difficult days, perhaps the most difficult a man can undergo. The dead are lucky, it's all over for them. I think of you constantly with heartfelt love and gratitude. Perhaps all will yet be well and we shall see each other again."
Erwin Rommel, letter to his wife, November 1, 1942

The British in Burma

"Wingate seemed to me hardly sane—in medical jargon a borderline case."

Diary of Lord Moran, Churchill's personal physician

The Japanese wanted Burma for its rubber, oil, and rice. For the British it was the gateway to India, their richest imperial possession. Moreover, since 1938, the Burma Road from Mandalay to Kunming had been the only overland supply route for the Nationalist forces fighting the Japanese in China.

On December 9, 1941, China joined the Allies, declaring war on Germany, Italy, and Japan—a formality long overdue. US General Joseph W. Stilwell joined the nationalist commander-in-chief Chiang Kai-shek as his chief of staff.

They repulsed a sustained attack in China by the Japanese on January 15, 1942. That day the Japanese, who had already moved into Burma from Thailand (with whom they had signed a treaty of friendship), began to bomb the capital Rangoon, which was evacuated. On April 29, the Japanese took Lasio, cutting the Burma Road. After that, the Chinese had to be supplied by air "over the Hump"—that is, the Himalayas. Faced with Japanese superiority in the air and on the ground, the remains of the British Burma Corps fled back to Imphal in India before the monsoon broke in May 1942. The monsoon halted the Japanese, but the British had found they had other troubles. There were independence protests in eastern India, and a famine in Bengal claimed three million lives. The British Army there was also starved of materiel due to the Anglo-American "Germany First" policy. Nevertheless, in December, the Indian Army managed to reoccupy the Mayu Peninsula and Akyab Island on the Burmese coast, which had a port and airfield vital for the reconquest of Burma.

THE CHINDITS

Meanwhile Brigadier Charles Orde Wingate formed a long-range penetration group of British, Gurkha, and Burmese irregulars. Their aim was to cause disruption behind enemy lines, communicating by radio and being supplied from the air—innovations at the time. They took as their badge the mythical *chinthé*, the half-lion, half-griffin figure seen guarding Burmese pagodas. This gave them their name, Chindits. In China, Stillwell formed "Merrill's Marauders," trained by Orde Wingate along similar lines and commanded by Frank Dow Merrill.

CHARLES ORDE WINGATE

Before Orde Wingate was sent to Burma, he had organized night patrols in Palestine to defend Jewish settlements from Arab raiders. In January 1941, he was sent to head an Ethiopian–Sudanese force which ejected the Italians from Abyssinia and put Haile Selassie back on the throne. After training the Chindits and Merrill's Marauders, Orde Wingate commanded his men behind Japanese lines in Burma. He led airborne troops on an invasion of central Burma in March 1944, when he was killed in an airplane crash. Though British, Wingate's remains were buried in Arlington National Cemetery, Virginia.

Chindits in Burma
Members of General Orde Wingate's Allied commando force in Burma traveling through the jungle with their donkeys.

1943—Timeline

1943

ALLIES GAIN MOMENTUM

AS ALLIED STRATEGY BECAME MORE AND MORE EFFECTIVE, THERE WERE NO MORE VICTORIES FOR THE AXIS POWERS. THE BATTLE OF THE ATLANTIC WAS BEING WON, ALLOWING AMERICAN TROOPS TO BE SHIPPED SAFELY TO BRITAIN WHERE A HUGE INVASION FORCE WAS BEGINNING TO BE ASSEMBLED. THE BOMBING OF GERMANY WAS STEPPED UP, AND A DARING RAID WAS MADE AGAINST THE HYDROELECTRIC DAMS THAT SUPPLIED WATER AND POWER TO GERMANY'S INDUSTRIAL HEARTLAND, THE RUHR.

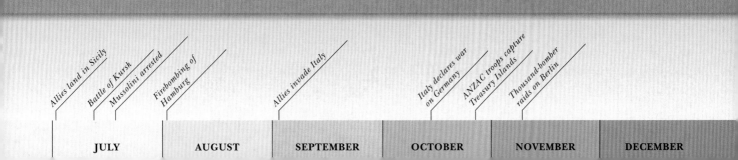

Allies land in Sicily

Battle of Kursk

Mussolini arrested

Firebombing of Hamburg

Allies invade Italy

Italy declares war on Germany

ANZAC troops capture Treasury Islands

Thousand-bomber raids on Berlin

| JULY | AUGUST | SEPTEMBER | OCTOBER | NOVEMBER | DECEMBER |

"SOFT UNDERBELLY"

The Germans were finally forced out of North Africa in a pincer movement where the American Army was first bloodied at the Kasserine Pass, then triumphant once Patton had taken over. This left the way open for an Anglo-American force to landed on Sicily. It was part of Churchill's plan to avoid landing in northern France, favored by the US, and attack Europe through its "soft underbelly." That way, Churchill believed, the Western Allies could race up the Italian Peninsula and invade Germany before the Red Army could get there. With the invasion of Sicily, Mussolini fell from power but was rescued and reinstated as a puppet ruler in the north. Germany simply assumed control of its former ally Italy and German soldiers committed atrocities against Italian civilians, as well as servicemen, for "betraying them."

HITLER TAKES COMMAND

On the Eastern Front, the Red Army inflicted a devastating defeat on the Germans at Stalingrad. They beat them again at Kursk in the biggest tank battle ever fought. Although Hitler believed that Slavs were inferior to the Aryan Germans, no matter what he did he could not turn them back. In the early years of the war he left the planning to his commanders, such as the Panzer pioneer General Heinz Guderian. Now he took command himself. He used the old tactics that had worked well, in the hands of others, at the beginning of the war. But the situation had changed. His enemies knew what to expect and had developed new weapons to thwart him. Even his own men were beginning to have their doubts.

A TERRIBLE PRICE

In the Pacific the Japanese would find themselves in full retreat. After America had won the major sea battles, Japan could no longer supply its armed forces scattered across the Pacific. Fanatical Japanese soldiers were still willing—if not eager—to give their lives for their emperor, but they found themselves abandoned and starving. The Axis nations, who had been sure of victory when they had started the war, were now assured of defeat. Over the next two-and-half years they would have to pay a terrible price.

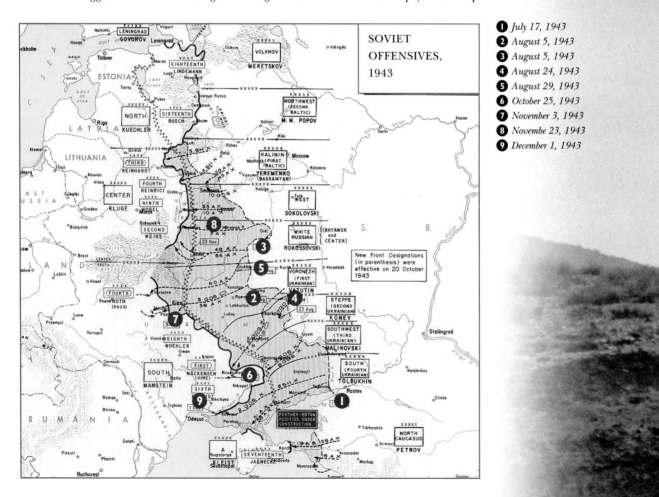

SOVIET OFFENSIVES, 1943

❶ *July 17, 1943*
❷ *August 5, 1943*
❸ *August 5, 1943*
❹ *August 24, 1943*
❺ *August 29, 1943*
❻ *October 25, 1943*
❼ *November 3, 1943*
❽ *Novembe 23, 1943*
❾ *December 1, 1943*

Americans in the Pacific (LEFT)
US Marines storm Kiribati's capital,
Tarawa, in the Gilbert Islands,
Pacific Ocean, 1942.

Desert triumph (BELOW)
US soldiers pilot an M3 General Grant tank,
North Africa, 1942.

Island hopping

"Our armament must be adequate to the needs, but our faith is not primarily in these machines of defense but in ourselves."

Admiral Chester W. Nimitz, Commander-in-Chief, US Pacific Fleet

The US strategy was to make amphibious assaults on island after island across the Pacific, until American forces were within bombing range of Japan's home islands, then within range to mount an assault on the home islands themselves. It was a costly strategy in men and materiel. But the Marines never turned back, and island hopping was ultimately successful. The atomic bomb attacks were made from the island of Tinian, captured in July 1944.

Moving between islands (ABOVE)
A US tank with infantry escort moves through the jungle, Bougainville, Papua New Guinea, 1943.

Carrier force (ABOVE)
An F6F fighter aircraft prepares for take-off aboard USS Yorktown, *1943.*

Pacific advance (RIGHT)
USS Iowa *fires her main batteries during a battle drill in the Pacific, 1944.*

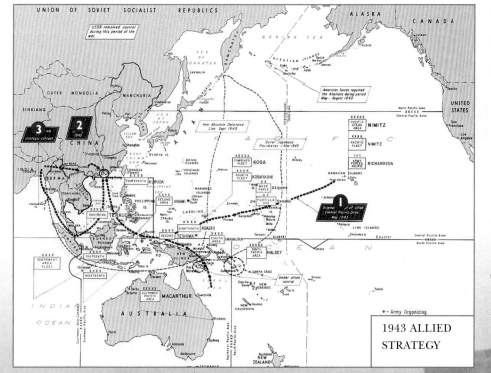

1 *Original concept of Allied Control Pacific Drive, May 1943*

2 *Allied strategic objectives, May 1943*

3 *British role in strategic concept*

Closing in (BELOW)
US soldiers head for the Japanese island of Iwo Jima, 1943.

Surrender at Stalingrad

"Imagine Stalingrad, eighty days and nights of hand-to-hand fighting. The streets are no longer measured in meters, but in corpses. Stalingrad is no longer a town. By day it is an enormous cloud of burning, blinding smoke. It is a vast furnace lit by the reflection of the flames."

A German veteran

By January 1943, it was clear that the German Sixth Army under General Paulus was going to endure another winter in the Soviet Union. Meanwhile, the morale of the Russians received a boost. Gold epaulettes from the pre-revolutionary era were distributed, the regimental traditions of the imperial army were revived, and political interference by commissars ceased. Soldiers were now fighting for Mother Russia, not the Communist Party.

Forty thousand Russians held a strip of the city barely ten miles long. At its widest it reached a mile-and-a-quarter inland from the west bank of the Volga river, at its narrowest 500

yards. Defending the city were hardened troops who knew every cellar, sewer, crater, and ruin of this wasteland, and they waited with machine guns and sniper rifles. Against them were pitched veteran German troops, who were demoralized by the losses they had taken, or raw recruits unprepared for the horrors they were about to face. Although the Soviet artillery fire was growing steadily heavier, Hitler announced that Stalingrad would fall "very shortly" and Paulus planned a fourth all-out offensive. Before he could launch it the Russians counterattacked, inflicting many casualties.

THE GERMAN OFFENSIVE

On October 14, two new German armored divisions and five infantry divisions pushed forward on a front just three miles wide, but they found the city blocks, or squares, heavily mined. The Russians fought house by house, floor by floor. That day, General Vasily Chuikov, the general in charge of the defense of Stalingrad, said was "the bloodiest and most ferocious day of the whole battle." The Soviets were pushed back so close to the Volga that boats bringing supplies across the river came under heavy machine-gun fire.

At the last moment a Siberian division was introduced into the battle. Its men were told to fight to the death. They were pounded with German mortars, artillery, and dive-bombers. Over the next two weeks the Germans made 117 separate attacks—23 on a single day. But the Siberians held out. Stalled, the Germans took to the sewers for the last 300 yards under the city to the Volga. But when they reached it, they were cut off. There was hand-to-hand combat under the rubble. After four days, only Russians were left. Then a terrible silence fell over Stalingrad—the silence of death.

GERMAN SIXTH ARMY DESTROYED

"What was destroyed at Stalingrad was the flower of the German Wehrmacht. Hitler was particularly proud of the Sixth Army and its great striking power. Under von Reichmann it was the first to invade Belgium. It entered Paris. It took part in the invasion of Yugoslavia and Greece. Before the war it had taken part in the occupation of Czechoslovakia. In 1942 it broke through from Kharkov to Stalingrad."
Red Star, the Red Army newspaper, February 5, 1943

Battle for Stalingrad (LEFT)
Red Army troops under German fire run for cover, 1943.

Soviet victory (ABOVE)
German soldiers and equipment captured, USSR, 1943.

THE GERMANS ENCIRCLED

By that time, General Georgii Zhukov—who had been defending Moscow—had built up a new army. Soviet guns opened up to the north and south of the city. A pincer movement quickly encircled 250,000 Germans in the most decisive breakthrough on the Eastern Front. Hitler ordered General Paulus to hold his ground until "Fortress Stalingrad" was relieved.

Göring informed Hitler that his Luftwaffe could fly in 500 tons of stores a day. Meanwhile, General Erich von Manstein rushed to the rescue with a spearhead of Panzer tanks leading a convoy of supply trucks. He was halted by Soviet T34 tanks, and Paulus refused to try to break out, because Hitler had ordered him to stay where he was. Göring failed to live up to his promise of air supplies.

On January 8, the Russians offered terms. Hitler promoted Paulus to Field Marshal to pressure him not to accept. On January 30, Paulus's command post was overrun and 91,000 freezing and hungry survivors were captured. As the Germans were marched away, a Soviet colonel pointed at the rubble of Stalingrad and shouted: "That's how Berlin is going to look." Two entire German armies were wiped out, including their reserves. Some 300,000 trained men had been lost. They were irreplaceable. The battle had been a bloodbath. In the last stages alone, 147,200 Germans and 46,700 Russians had been killed.

The "Dambusters" raid

"What kind of a war is this? General, this is not war—this is sheer madness."

Leipzig firefighter returning from duty in Hamburg, August 1943

The Area Bombing Campaign was going well. On March 12, 1943, Air Minister Sir Archibald Sinclair told the House of Commons that in the "Battle of the Ruhr" 2,000 factories had been wrecked, one million tons of steel lost, and coal production was down by 20 percent. The RAF now planned a devastating blow by destroying the dams that supplied hydroelectric power to German industry.

Four hundred acres of Düsseldorf had already been razed. A 1,000-ton raid on Essen had destroyed 30 engineering workshops. One bomb set off an explosion that sent a sheet of flame shooting 1,000 feet into the air. But German war output continued rising. Then, on the night of May 17, the specially modified Lancaster bombers of the RAF's 617 Squadron, led by Wing Commander Guy Gibson, attacked the Möhne and Eder dams using "bouncing bombs" designed by British aeronautical engineer Barnes Wallis. These circular, rotating bombs, dropped low, skipped over the surface of the water and exploded while sinking to the foot of the dam. A 100-yard breach was opened in the Möhne dam, while the Eder, the largest dam in Europe— it held back a 17-mile reservoir—was

Mission accomplished (BELOW)
The Möhne Dam, destroyed by British bombers ("The Dambusters"), 1943.

destroyed along with its power station. Walls of water swept down the Ruhr and Eder valleys, killing at least 1,500 people, flooding mines and steelworks, and forcing people to flee to higher ground.

THE FIREBOMBING OF HAMBURG

Over eight days in the summer of 1943, from July 27 to August 3, the RAF by night and the USAAF by day dropped 10,000 tons of bombs over Hamburg, demolishing seven square miles of Germany's second city, including the dockyards and submarines on their slipways. After a lull of two days, the bombers attacked the city again on the night of August 6, this time with new phosphorous incendiaries that set fire to asphalt, turning the streets into rivers of fire. A second wave of bombers was guided by the fires. The aptly-named "Operation Gomorrah" caused firestorms that sucked people into the flames and burned people to death in their air-raid shelters. At least 50,000 people died. Hamburg was bombed another 69 times before the end of the war.

Hero of the hour (ABOVE)
Wing Commander Guy Gibson autographs a map
showing the location of the Möhne Resevoir area, 1943.

THE EFFECT OF INCENDIARY BOMBS

"Outside all was a sea of flames. The house next to ours was in flames. You couldn't see that there were any flames in our house because of the air-raid curtains. It was difficult to get to my house because of the air raid and across the way a house had had a direct hit and was blocking the entrance somewhat. I got inside and ran upstairs. As I got in, a wave of smoke met me. Several incendiary bombs had penetrated the attic. I threw sand on them and extinguished them. Also a bed had caught on fire. I threw it out of the window. I had to go downstairs then because it was difficult to breathe up there …"
Survivor of an incendiary bomb attack

Afrika Korps surrenders

"General von Arnim, as commander of the Axis forces in Tunisia, took the opportunity to express Field Marshall Kesselring's approval and, disregarding the proximity of the enemy, he decorated some of our valiant fighters in the most advanced line …"

Colonel Rudolf Lang

The Axis forces in North Africa in 1942 were now caught. Field Marshal Rommel was being pursued across the Libyan desert by the cautious General Montgomery, who was determined not to fall into the traps of the "Desert Fox" like previous British commanders. To Rommel's rear, there was another Allied force about to push from Algeria.

After landing at Algiers, the British First Army moved down the coast toward Tunis on November 23, 1942. Ten miles over the Tunisian border, it was attacked by troops under General Walther Nehring who had air superiority and forced the British back. In December the British tried again to head for Tunis, but they were met by the German Fifth Army under Nehring's replacement General Jurgen von Arnim and were pushed back once more. By then Rommel had been forced out of Libya and was occupying the Mareth Line, a series of fortifications built by the French before the war. He persuaded von Arnim to hit the US Second Corps frontally at the Kasserine Pass, while his Afrika Korps attacked their flank at Gafsa on February 14, 1943. The inexperienced American troops were badly bloodied. They lost over 2,000 men of which 1,400 were taken prisoner, including General Patton's son-in-law, Lieutenant Colonel John Waters. But von Arnim was in command and did not exploit the situation. Rommel took over.

Transporting prisoners (ABOVE)
German POWs captured in Africa prepare for embarkation, Algiers, 1943.

PATTON AND MONTGOMERY

On February 26, Rommel pushed the British First Army back, but suffered unsustainable casualties and broke off his assult. He then attacked Montgomery's Eighth Army south of the Mareth Line, losing a third of his tanks. Three days later, a sick man, Rommel left Africa, leaving the Afrika Korps under the command of Field Marshall Albrecht Kesselring. Patton took over the US Second Corps and reorganized it along the lines of Montgomery's Eighth Army. Montgomery then made a frontal assault on the Mareth Line, while Patton launched a diversionary assault on Gafsa. The New Zealand Division drove around the flank of the Mareth Line, forcing the Afrika Korps to abandon its position. Axis forces then fell back to a small enclave around Tunis. They were told to fight until the last bullet, but many shot in the air. The city fell to the British on May 7. Over 250,000 German prisoners were taken. The whole of Africa was now in Allied hands.

Americans push ahead (BELOW)
US artillery and jeep escort outside Haldra, Tunisia, 1943.

SHERMAN TANK CAPTURED

"Through the streets of Tunis rolls an American Sherman tank—bouncing along on its mobile tracks, its engine rumbling, with captured ammunition in its gun barrels, and on board, its crew—the German scout patrol that captured it in the hills of Sbeitla on the foggy morning of February 22. Down it travels from the hills through the sea of olive groves, headed towards the seaport of Sfax. It's a journey of some 210 miles, lasting four-and-a-half days, which testifies well to the overall march capacity of this steel colossus. The thing weighs about 31 metric tons. It was loaded onto a ship in the harbor while German fighter planes wheeled overhead in the clear sky of Africa, and not one enemy bomber dared intrude on this deadly zone. Now, after many intermediate stops, this star of American armament has arrived at its destination, a proving ground near Berlin, in the hands of German arms experts who are testing its combat efficiency and durability. Preliminary investigation in Tunisia had already revealed that this rolling steelmine is not a bad product. It was captured by a German Panzer regiment."
The March issue of the German Army newspaper Die Wehrmacht, announcing the capture of an American tank

The Battle of Kursk

"At this time, Hitler's propaganda was still strong, telling us 'just one more push and the Russians will collapse forever'."

Herbert Winckelmann, on being sent back to the Eastern Front in November 1943

Despite their defeat at Stalingrad in January 1943, in the summer of that year, the Germans tried to seize the initiative in the Soviet Union once more. A huge salient 150 miles wide had developed around Kursk, with the Soviet lines protruding 100 miles westward into the German lines. The scene was now set for the largest tank battle in history.

On April 15, 1943, Hitler ordered Operation *Zitadelle*—"Citadel"—to "encircle the enemy and annihilate them." His generals were against it. Panzer pioneer General Heinz Guderian urged that tanks be preserved against the Allied landings expected in 1944, while General Walther Model, commander of the German Ninth Army on the Eastern Front, pointed out that the Russians were prepared for a German pincer movement, because spies in the German High Command had informed them of the plan. But Hitler insisted that the assault go ahead "for political reasons." By June 15, the Germans had assembled an assault force of 50 divisions—900,000 men—with 17 armored divisions, boasting 2,700 tanks and mobile assault guns. Ahead of them were 400,000 mines laid so they would channel the armor into nests of anti-tank guns. The Soviets had deployed 6,000 anti-tank guns, 20,000 other artillery pieces, howitzers and mortars, and 920 rocket launchers. They outnumbered the Gemans with 75 divisions and 3,600 tanks. In all, two million men were involved, supported by 4,000 aircraft.

HEAVIER THAN VERDUN

The German offensive was delayed until July 5, allowing the Russians more time to prepare their defenses. Some twenty minutes before zero hour the Soviets bombarded the German assembly points. By the evening of the first day the Panzers had advanced only six miles through the Soviet defenses. The northern thrust of their pincer movement was halted on the second day just 12 miles from the start line. The southern arm managed to penetrate 20 miles and, eight days into the battle, it had taken 24,000 prisoners and destroyed or captured 100 tanks and 108 anti-tank guns. Even so, the gap between the two jaws of the pincer movement was still 75 miles. On July 12, the Soviets launched an offensive against the salient created around Orel to the north. Hitler had already lost 20,000 men. His offensive had stalled. Now he had to withdraw troops to defend Orel. The Allies had landed on Sicily on July 10 and German troops would have to be sent to southern Italy. Hitler called a halt to Zitadelle. The Soviets now opened an artillery barrage that was "ten times heavier than at Verdun," clearing the German minefields. Overhead there were huge air battles with heavy losses on both sides. But after three days the Red Army broke through. Behind the German lines partisans began blowing up the railroads to prevent supplies and reinforcements reaching the front. Nothing could halt the Soviet onslaught. While the Germans lost men as they pulled back, the Red Army gained conscripts with every mile they took. The German Army fought on for nearly another two years but, after Kursk, there was nothing they could do to prevent the Red Army driving forward all the way to Berlin.

Aerial attack
Soviet tanks at Kursk come under fire from German Stuka dive bombers, 1943.

The Soviets advance

"The greatest delight is to mark one's enemy, prepare everything,

avenge oneself thoroughly, and then go to sleep."

Joseph Stalin

After the battle of Kursk in July 1943, there was no hope of winning for the Germans in the East. They were confronted with the T-34, a tank that was superior to their Panzers and which the Soviets could turn out in greater numbers. The Blitzkrieg tactics that the Germans had used in the early part of the war only worked when an army was on the offensive. They were no good if an army was on the retreat. The Germans resorted to World War I tactics, attempting to establish a series of static defensive lines. But warfare had moved on and these were easily overwhelmed.

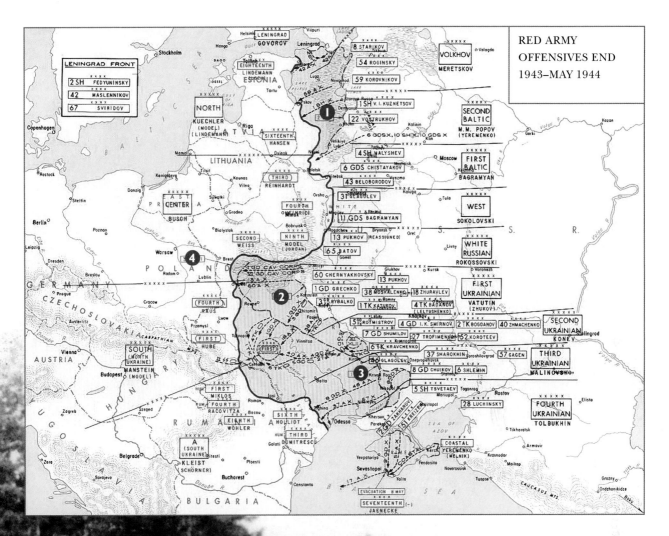

RED ARMY OFFENSIVES END 1943–MAY 1944

LENINGRAD FRONT

2 SH	FEDYUNINSKY
42	MASLENNIKOV
67	SVIRIDOV

KEY OPERATIONS

1. *December 2, 1944*
2. *December 2, 1944*
3. *1 March, 1944*
4. *30 April, 1944*

Stalingrad holds (INSET)
German soldiers attempt to hold back Soviet troops, 1943.

Soviets on the move (LEFT)
A Soviet tank makes its way towards the Western Front, 1943.

The war comes to Italy

"We pull out in the morning for the invasion of Sicily. I think it will be a pretty bloody show ... I doubt that I will be killed or even wounded, but one can never tell. It is all a question of destiny."

General George S. Patton, letter to his wife Beatrice, July 9, 1943

At a meeting in Casablanca, western Morocco, in January 1943, Churchill had persuaded Roosevelt that, after North Africa, they should attack the "soft underbelly" of Europe—Sicily. However, in an elaborate deception, a body in a Royal Marine uniform was dropped in the waters off Spain with papers suggesting the attacks would be on Sardinia. The Spanish handed the papers to the Germans, who were taken in by the ruse. Hitler ordered the strengthening of fortifications on Sardinia and Corsica. A Panzer division was sent to Greece and two more withdrawn from the Soviet Union, immediately before the conflict at Kursk.

THE ALLIES LAND IN SICILY

On July 10, 1943, at 05:00 hours, Montgomery's Eighth Army and General Patton's Seventh Army landed on the southern shores of Sicily to find the island's defenders were drawn up along the north shore, facing Sardinia. They knew an attack was coming. For a month, their defenses had been pounded by 4,000 Allied planes. In response, the defenders could put up just 200 Italian and 320 German planes, and much of the island's infrastructure, including its airfields, had been wiped out. Even so, the landings were nearly a disaster. Axis aircraft had spotted the Allied fleet leaving Malta. The fleet was hit by a storm, nearly forcing it to turn back. In the heavy weather, the defenders dropped their guard, but high winds took their toll on the invading airborne troops, blowing gliders and parachutists out to sea to their deaths. Those that landed on the island were widely dispersed. Nevertheless, they succeeded in harassing enemy movements, and 100 British airborne troops took a vital bridge on the coast road and held it for five days until the Eighth Army arrived.

THE AMPHIBIOUS ASSAULT

At dawn on July 10, the coastal defenses were pounded by tactical aircraft and naval gunfire. Then a fleet of 2,590 ships, including 237 troop transports and 1,742 landing craft, began putting ashore 115,000 British and Canadian troops, and 66,000 Americans. Facing them were the 230,000 men and 150 guns of the Italian Sixth Army and two Panzer divisions. The Italian coastal force put up a heroic defense but was virtually wiped out. The following morning the Panzers ran into the forward posts of the First American Division, but they came under fire from six Allied destroyers and the cruisers *Savannah* and *Boise*, who knocked out 30 German tanks. The Italian "Livorno" Division was also badly mauled. Meanwhile, the British Eighth Army occupied the ports of Augusta and Syracuse in the southeast without a shot being fired, because their garrisons had already been evacuated. On July 14, the airfields at Comiso and Ragusa in southern Sicily were taken and rapidly put back into commission.

PATTON AND MONTGOMERY RACE FOR MESSINA

The Allied dash was then on for Messina, the crossing point to mainland Italy. Once Messina was taken, the enemy would be trapped on the island and forced to surrender, but Field Marshal Albert Kesselring, now the German commander in Italy, preempted them. He sent in another Panzer division and General Hans Hube took over command of all German fighting forces in Sicily.

Montgomery's dash for Messina was stopped at Catania by stiff defense, halfway up the east coast. He then turned inland, switching his attack to the west of Mount Etna. But this move stepped on the Americans' toes. Patton pushed westward and captured Sicily's capital, Palermo, on July 22, 1943. He then began his own dash on Messina along the north coast. But

Hube stopped him at the small town of Santo Stefano, halfway down the coastal road. Meanwhile, the First Canadian Division pushed northwest, confining German defenders to the northeast corner of the island. The British were now landing the 78th Division at Syracuse, while the American Ninth Division landed at Palermo. This increased the Allies' strength to 11 divisions. Totally outnumbered, Hube pulled back.

MUSSOLINI'S DOWNFALL

On the night of July 24, Mussolini told the Grand Council of Fascists that the Germans were thinking of evacuating southern Italy. Hitler was clearly more interested in defending Germany than Italy and, after the reverses on the Eastern Front, some members of the Grand Council believed that his defeat was inevitable. Their priority was to prevent Italy from becoming a battleground. They voted against Mussolini, who was arrested and imprisoned at Campo Imperatore, high in the Abruzzi mountains. Meanwhile, the new Italian government, led by Marshal Pietro Badoglio, began secret peace talks with the Allies, while assuring the Germans that

Long live the king
Civilians and soldiers read that Mussolini has been deposed and the Italian king reinstated, Italy, 1943.

they were doing nothing of the sort. After the fall of Mussolini, Kesselring was ordered by Hitler to withdraw from Sicily. The Strait of Messina was bristling with anti-aircraft guns and Hube managed to get two-thirds of his force across to the Italian mainland before, at 08:30 hours on August 17, 1943, the British and Americans met in the ruins of Messina, leaving just two miles of clear water between the Allied Army and the mainland. The invasion of Sicily cost 5,532 Allied dead, 14,410 wounded, and 2,869 missing. One destroyer was sunk and two cruisers damaged. The Italians lost 4,278 dead and the Germans 4,325. The Allies had taken some 132,000 prisoners, along with 520 guns and 260 tanks.

PATTON'S DISGRACE

After winning the race for Messina, "Old Blood and Guts" Patton snatched disaster from the jaws of triumph. Visiting the Allied wounded, he slapped two shell-shocked enlisted men, accusing them of cowardice. The press was outraged, but Eisenhower refused to sack him, saying: "Patton is indispensable to the war effort—one of the guarantors of our victory." However, Patton was forced to apologize and was ordered to remain behind in Palermo when the Allies invaded Italy. The final blow came when he heard that General Omar Bradley had been chosen to lead the US land forces in the invasion of Normandy.

The invasion of Italy

"A veil has been torn from a treacherous intrigue which for weeks had been enacted by an Italian clique, serfs to Jews and alien to their own people."

German propaganda broadcast on news of Italian capitulation

After the fall of Mussolini, the Allies began peace talks with the Italians. The new Italian government agreed to surrender terms the day the Allies landed on the mainland. But the Germans simply took over. While Italian resistance faded, the Germans tried to force the Allies back into the sea. When that failed they established a series of defensive lines up the peninsula that would stall the Allies for nearly two years. Churchill's strategy of attacking Hitler's Germany through the "soft underbelly of Europe" failed. He had aimed to race up the peninsula and cut Germany off from the advancing Red Army, but Allied troops had to fight ferocious battles every inch of the way.

A moment for reflection (BELOW)
A US soldier surveys the devastation of a bomb-damaged Catholic church, Italy, 1943.

Patton in conference (LEFT)
General George S. Patton discusses strategy with Lt. Col. Lyle Bernard, 1943.

Germans march on (ABOVE)
The 370th Infantry Division moves through Prato, Italy, 1943.

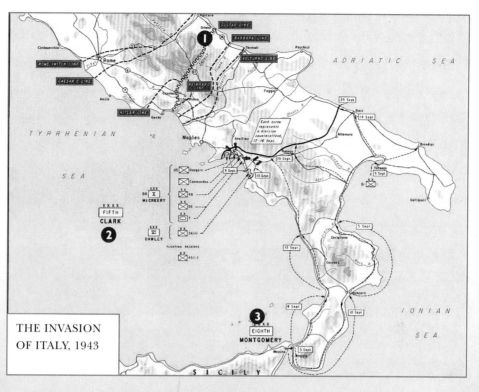

THE INVASION
OF ITALY, 1943

Battle for Monte Cassino (BELOW)
US tanks and escorts file towards the town of Cassino, Italy, 1943.

1 *The Gustav Line*
2 *Fifth Army under Clark*
3 *Eighth Army under Montgomery*

Italy changes sides

"All Italians who now act to help eject the German aggressor from Italian soil will have the assistance and support of the Allies."

Proclamation by General Dwight D. Eisenhower

On September 2, 1943, a small Allied force had landed on the "heel" of Italy, quickly taking the ports of Brindisi and Taranto. The following day, Montgomery's Eighth Army crossed the Strait of Messina and landed in Calabria, on the "toe" of Italy. That day, the new Italian government agreed to the Allied peace terms, though their capitulation was not announced until September 8.

Under the peace agreement, the Italian Navy was to surrender in Malta. On its way there, it was bombed by the Germans. German units also turned on the Italians in Greece and the Balkans, and disarmed them. On the Greek island of Cephalonia and in Croatia, two Italian divisions were massacred by German units. Italian survivors joined the Greek Resistance or Tito's partisans in Yugoslavia. In return for Italy's capitulation, the Americans had promised to land the 82nd Airborne Division on the outskirts of Rome and take over the city, but the Third Panzergrenadier Division got there first. On September 9, an Anglo-American force under General Mark Clark landed at the beachhead of Salerno, 30 miles south of Naples. Kesselring had anticipated this move and managed to hold the Allies back in their bridgehead for six days.

GERMANY INVADES

Hitler had anticipated the fall of Mussolini and sent 17 more divisions into Italy under the command of Rommel, who set up his headquarters in Bologna on August 17, 1943. Several Italian units melted away, but Rommel managed to take over ten divisions and add them to his command. Effectively, Italy had been invaded by Germany and Hitler even threatened to arrest the king. On September 12, Kesselring counterattacked between the British and American forces, attempting then to encircle and crush the American beachhead at Salerno. Clark threw every man he had into the fight, including a regimental band, orderlies, and cooks. But Hitler denied Kesselring reinforcements and the German advance foundered under a naval bombardment just five miles from the beach. New German radio-controlled bombs hit the US cruiser *Savannah*, as well as the British cruiser *Uganda* and the battleship *Warspite*, which had been brought close to the coast. Eventually

Allied landings
US troops land on the Italian mainland near Salerno, 1943.

the Americans were relieved when Montgomery broke through at Agropoli. On October 1 the American Fifth Army entered Naples, while more British forces landed at Bari and Termoli on the Adriatic coast. The German Tenth Army had been defeated at a cost of 5,674 American casualties.

ITALY CHANGES SIDES

On October 13, 1943, the new Italian government in Rome declared war on Germany. This did not bother Kesselring unduly because German reinforcements were already consolidating their hold on north and central Italy, where a new Fascist republic had been set up under Benito Mussolini, who had been rescued from prison in a daring raid. The Repubblica Sociale Italiana was established on September 18 at Salò on Lake Garda. Members of the Grand Council of Fascists who had voted against Mussolini, including his own son-in-law, former Foreign Minister Count Ciano, were arrested and executed. But otherwise, as Mussolini himself admitted, he was merely a puppet. None of the neutral countries—not even Fascist Spain—would recognize Mussolini's new republic. In Rome Marshal Ugo Cavallero committed suicide rather than accept Kesselring's offer of the command of a new Fascist army.

The Italian declaration of war followed a wave of atrocities and looting after Italy's surrender. In Rome, German troops stole priceless manuscripts and artifacts. Civilians in Naples had been subjected to a five-day reign of terror by the retreating Germans. In one case, they herded 100 Neapolitans into a room and blew it up with land mines. Hospitals were attacked, food stocks stolen, water mains and sewers dynamited. In villages across the country, Germans murdered Italians at random, claiming that they had betrayed them. Meanwhile, tens of thousands of disarmed Italian soldiers were packed into sealed trains and taken to Germany as slave labor. But in the south the Germans were facing another foe who was not nearly as helpless.

AN ITALIAN PILOT'S STORY

"We decided, a few families, a few friends, to go over to the Allies. But there were minefields everywhere. The Yankee or British Navy, I don't know, were shelling these big towers. There were Germans there. I know this because I helped them. I didn't want to. I had to. Otherwise I would be shot. Then I became a bit of a devil. I couldn't care less what happened to me in those days. A German came and pointed the gun on me and said: 'I will shoot.' I said: 'You shoot, you bastard, if you like.' You know you become like that when you see so much suffering."
Antonio Colette, Italian Air Force

THE GUSTAV LINE

Rommel's Panzers checked the American Fifth Army on the Volturno river, just 20 miles north of Naples. But Rommel was urged by Hitler to abandon Rome and withdraw to the north. On November 21, Rommel was relieved. On the east coast, the British advance had run out of steam when the roads through the mountainous terrain became jammed with vehicles. French colonial troops arrived with horses and mules instead. The Germans dug in for the winter along the Gustav Line, a defensive position that ran for 100 miles across the Italian peninsula which hinged on the town of Cassino with the historic Benedictine monastery of Monte Cassino on the mountain above it.

Berlin bombed

"The Battle of Berlin progresses. It will continue as opportunity serves and circumstances dictate, until the heart of Nazi Germany ceases to beat."

Air Marshal Sir Arthur "Bomber" Harris, November 25, 1943

Although the RAF had bombed Berlin during the night of August 25, 1940, provoking the Blitz, it was not one of the target cities selected in the Area Bombing Directive of February 14, 1942. However, for the sake of morale, it was plain that raids on the German capital were vital. The RAF proposed to give Berlin the same treatment that London had suffered.

The bombings began with two daring daylight raids by RAF Mosquito fighter-bombers on January 31, 1943. The first was timed to strike just as Hitler's deputy and head of the Luftwaffe Reichsmarschall Hermann Göring was to deliver a radio broadcast, celebrating ten years of Nazi rule. Surprised by the lack of anti-aircraft flak—the Germans had not been prepared for a daylight raid—one Mosquito pilot said: "I imagine all the gunners were tuned into Göring and they had left their posts." The second raid came that afternoon, just as Propaganda Minister Joseph Goebbels took the microphone.

THOUSAND-BOMBER RAIDS

In November, Bomber Command began pounding Berlin with thousand-bomber raids, each dropping 2,500 tons of high explosives. By January 20, 1944, 17,000 tons of bombs had been dropped on Berlin, reducing it to rubble. That night, a Swedish correspondent reported that the sirens went off at 19:00 hours. Within minutes the first bombs were falling. In just over half an hour, 600 Lancaster and Halifax bombers dropped 2,300 tons of bombs, starting 30 major fires. The 3,000-foot cloud of smoke was so thick that the huge four-engined bombers had to dive through it and deliver their bombs from a few hundred feet

above ground. After one attack on Berlin with incendiaries, RAF pilots said the flames could be seen 200 miles away. In all there were 363 air raids on Berlin by Bomber Command and the USAAF Eighth Air Force. An estimated 20,000 people were killed, many more injured, and hundreds of thousands rendered homeless.

BERLIN UNDER ATTACK

"I did not even hear the air-raid sirens and did not wake until a window shattered about two o'clock in the morning. I jumped from my bed to witness the horror of an air raid over Berlin … Although I could not see the planes, I could hear their continuous grumbling above me. They unloaded their bombs on the north side of town which became a burning inferno. Our searchlights sweeping the sky illuminated it like a dome. Occasionally they caught a plane in their cross lights and our anti-aircraft guns would roar into full blast and the plane unable to escape would burst into flames and fall to the ground. It was clear to me that our furniture had to be moved out of Berlin for safekeeping, but bigoted Nazis still maintained that Berlin was a safe town."
Herbert Winkelmann, at home in Berlin on leave from the Eastern Front

Fires over Germany (LEFT)
A Lancaster bomber, surrounded by trails of dropped bombs, 1943.

Daring raids (INSET)
The B-17 Flying Fortress bomber specialized in daylight attacks..

1944–Timeline

Siege of Leningrad lifted

Battle of Anzio

The "Great Escape"

Red Army
retakes Crimea

Fortress Europe

Monte Cassino

Rome falls to the Allies

D-Day

Battle of the Philippine
Sea

JANUARY   FEBRUARY   MARCH   APRIL   MAY   JUNE

1944
THE ALLIES CLOSE IN

IN THE EARLY DAYS OF THE WAR, EVERYTHING SEEMED TO GO THE WAY OF THE AXIS POWERS. BUT BY THE BEGINNING OF 1944, THEY HAD BEEN SUFFERING CATASTROPHIC DEFEATS FOR A YEAR. ALTHOUGH MUSSOLINI CLUNG ON IN HIS NEW REPUBBLICA SOCIALE ITALIANA, THE ITALIAN ARMY PLAYED NO MORE PART IN THE WAR, WHILE ITALIAN PARTISANS HARASSED THE GERMANS BEHIND THEIR LINES. GERMANY AND JAPAN COULD NO LONGER MATCH THE FORCES SET AGAINST THEM.

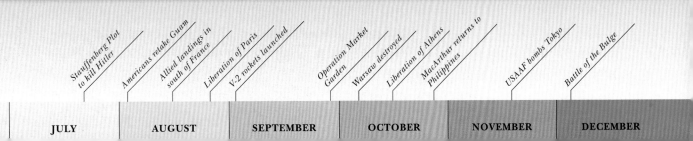

Stauffenberg Plot to kill Hitler

Americans retake Guam

Allied landings in south of France

Liberation of Paris

V-2 rockets launched

Operation Market Garden

Warsaw destroyed

Liberation of Athens

MacArthur returns to Philippines

USAAF bombs Tokyo

Battle of the Bulge

| JULY | AUGUST | SEPTEMBER | OCTOBER | NOVEMBER | DECEMBER |

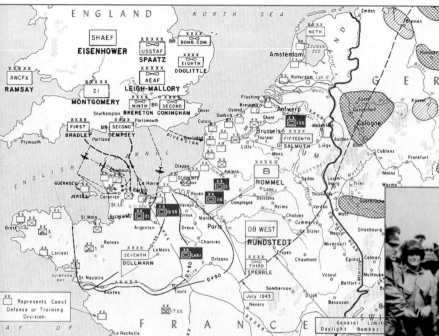

Preparing for battle (LEFT)
*Map shows line-up of Allied and
German forces in England and
Northern France before D-Day.*

Allies invade France (BELOW)
*US General Dwight D. Eisenhower
speaks to American paratroopers on
the eve of the Normandy D-Day
landings, June 5, 1944.*

Nothing could halt the relentless advance of the Red Army as it
rolled through the Ukraine. As the Germans pulled back, the
900-day siege of Leningrad was lifted. In the south, the Soviets
retook the Crimea. However, they paused just long enough
outside Warsaw to let the Germans destroy the city and, with it,
any opposition to the new Communist government that Stalin
intended to install in Poland. The Germans had behaved so
brutally during their invasion of the USSR that they feared the
retribution they might receive at Soviet hands. Senior German
army officers decided that the only hope was to kill those
responsible—Hitler, Göring, and Himmler—and make peace.
Their assassination attempt failed. They paid with their lives.

THE FAR EAST

In the Pacific, the US continued its strategy of island hopping.
It was costly in terms of the lives of Marines, but General
Douglas MacArthur fulfilled his earlier promise and returned
to the Philippines. By the end of the year, US forces were close
enough to the Japanese home islands for the USAAF to begin
a bombing campaign that would devastate Japanese cities.
Meanwhile, the British began clearing the Japanese out of
Burma, while the Australians did the same in Borneo.

THE NORMANDY LANDINGS

In western Europe, Allied progress up the Italian Peninsula
was painfully slow. New landings at Anzio, fewer than 40 miles
from Rome, did not help when the offensive stalled at the

beachhead. It was over four months before the Germans
evacuated Rome and the city fell. But, all the time, the greatest
amphibious assault in history was being prepared. On June 6,
1944—D-Day—British, Canadian, and American soldiers
landed on the Normandy coast in massive strength. Again they
were stalled at the beachhead. But once they broke out, much
of the Germany Army in France was encircled and annihilated.
As the Allied forces raced toward Germany, the British
overextended themselves and were soundly defeated at
Arnhem in the Netherlands. This raised German spirits
enough for them to stage a counteroffensive in the Ardennes,
which failed. Although it was now clear even to Hitler that he
could not win, he sought revenge with his new "vengeance
weapons," the V-1 flying bomb and V-2 ballistic missile. They
rained down on London, which had suffered the Blitz four
years before. Hitler even had plans to attack New York. He
believed that if he could inflict enough damage, the western
Allies would seek to make peace. In his wildest fantasies, he
believed that they might be persuaded to change sides and
join him fighting the Soviets. The man was, as ever, deluded.

Normandy landings (LEFT)
*Allied troops disembark en masse in
Normandy, France, 1944.*

The Warsaw Uprising (BELOW)
*Polish Home Army officer keeps
watch on the ruined streets of
Warsaw, 1944.*

The Eastern Front

"The arrogant invaders run like rats, the ground hot beneath their feet. Destroy their ships. Shoot down their planes. Don't allow a single enemy to escape retribution."

Josef Stalin, Order of the Day, April 16, 1944

It was called the 900-day siege, though it lasted only 872 days. Starting in September 1941, the USSR's second-largest city, Leningrad was encircled by German and Finnish troops. The population was shelled and starved, but no matter what the Germans did they could not take the city. After the siege was lifted in January 1944, the city was awarded the Order of Lenin and named Hero City of the Soviet Union.

When Nazi Germany invaded the Soviet Union in June 1941, the Fourth Panzer Army made a northerly thrust through the Baltic states while their Finnish allies approached from the north down the Karelian Isthmus. As the Germans made their final assault on Leningrad in early August, the city's 200,000 defenders counterattacked, pushing the Germans back, and its entire population was mobilized to build anti-tank fortifications. The German High Command then decided to besiege the city rather than storm it, because their tanks could be better used in the attack on Moscow. Meanwhile, the Finns halted on the 1939 Russo–Finnish border and could not be prevailed upon to go any further. On September 1, the Germans began bombarding Leningrad, besieging it on September 8th. By November the city was completely encircled and 11,000 people had died in the fighting. Vital rail and other overland supply lines were cut, and ice made Lake Ladoga unnavigable.

Red Army in the Crimea
German troops flee from approaching Soviet forces in the Crimea, USSR, 1944.

THE ENEMY AT THE GATE

"The moment has come to put your Bolshevik qualities to work, to get ready to defend Leningrad without wasting words. We have to see that nobody is just an onlooker, and carry out in the least possible time the same kind of mobilization of the workers that was done in 1918 and 1919. The enemy is at the gate. It is a question of life and death."
A. A. Zhdanov, head of the local Communist Party committee

STARVATION

During the siege, 630,000 Russians died of starvation, exposure, and disease. Another 200,000 Russians were killed by German bombardment. One million children, elderly, and sick were evacuated from the city. Sparse supplies of food and fuel reached it by barge during the summer, and by sled across the ice in winter. Vegetables were grown on all open ground and, somehow, the city's armament factories continued working. In the summer of 1943, Hitler planned to take Leningrad by storm, landing two divisions of paratroopers in the city, but the plan was shelved after the defeat at Kursk. The Russians made several attempts to relieve the city, but it was only in January 1944 that a concerted Russian attack on all fronts pushed the Germans back, raising the siege on January 27.

THE RUSSIANS RETAKE THE CRIMEA

In October 1941, the German Eleventh Army under Field Marshal Manstein had overrun the Crimea, except for Sebastopol and the Kerch Peninsula. The following May, Manstein launched another attack, led by dive-bombers, knocking out 200 tanks. One hundred thousand prisoners were taken and on July 7 the garrison in Sebastopol surrendered. But the Red Army would have its revenge.

In November 1943, General Fyodor Tolbukhin's drive along the northern shore of the Sea of Azov and the Black Sea cut off the German and Romanian troops in the Crimea. On April 11, 1944, three Russian armies thrust through the German defenses at the neck of the peninsula. The Black Sea port of Odessa fell almost immediately, leaving 5,500 Germans dead. The Red Army quickly retook Kerch to the east and Yalta to the south. By April 16, the Soviets had closed in on Sebastopol. The Germans were frantically trying to evacuate their forces by sea, but Russian dive-bombers took a dreadful toll on German ships, choking the harbor with wrecks and drowning thousands of people.

STREET FIGHTING

Heavy guns pounded Sebastopol, the city that had been a symbol of resistance—and the site of a year-long siege—during the Crimean War (1854–1856), some 90 years before. There was fighting in the streets, and the remains of nine German and Soviet divisions once 100,000-strong fought it out on the historic battlefields of Balaclava and Inkerman. The German garrison at Sebastopol finally surrendered on May 9 and 30,000 Germans were taken prisoner.

LANDINGS AT
ANZIO, 1944

Anzio

"I expected to see a wild cat roaring into the mountains—
and what do I find? A whale wallowing on the beaches."

Winston Churchill, in a letter to General Sir Harold Alexander

The road to Rome now blocked by Germans, the Allies staged another amphibious assault, On January 22, 1944, they landed 70,000 troops at Anzio and nearby Nettuno, just 37 miles south of Rome and 60 miles behind the Gustav Line. The aim was to cut German communications and force Kesselring to evacuate the Gustav Line, where the Allies were stalemated.

The idea of the landings at Anzio had come from Churchill. If the plan had worked, it would have proved his whole "soft underbelly" strategy. The Anglo-American force would have raced up the Italian Peninsula and into Germany before the Red Army got there. The landings were initially successful but the American commander, Major-General John P. Lucas, did not seize the opportunity to make a dash for Rome. Instead, he took the best part of a week to consolidate his bridgehead. This gave Kesselring time to mount a counteroffensive, effectively trapping the huge Anglo-American force in their bridgehead. Lucas tried to break out on January 30, but by then the Germans were strong enough to oppose him. Unable to move, Lucas was forced to established a static defense, which was pounded by a German 28cm railroad gun known variously as "Anzio Annie" or the "Anzio Express". With a barrel 135 feet long, it could hurl a 564-pound shell almost 40 miles, or a rocket-assisted shell over 50 miles.

SEALED OFF

On February 15, the Germans penetrated deep into the Allied positions and were only halted by a desperate American counterattack. The landing force remained sealed off until a general Allied advance on May 11 allowed Major-General

Lucien K. Truscott, Lucas's successor, to break out on May 23. According to the official US Navy account of Anzio: "It was the only amphibious operation in that theater where the Army was unable to promptly exploit a successful landing, or where the enemy contained Allied forces on a beachhead for a prolonged period. Indeed, in the entire war there is none to compare with it; even the Okinawa campaign in the Pacific was shorter."

TRAPPED ON THE BEACH

"I suppose that armchair strategists will always labor under the delusion that there was a 'fleeting opportunity' at Anzio during which some Napoleonic figure would have charged over the Colli Laziali, playing havoc with the German line of communications and galloping on into Rome. Any such concept betrays a lack of comprehension of the military problem involved. It was necessary to occupy the Corps Beachhead Line to prevent the enemy from interfering with the beaches, otherwise enemy artillery and armored detachments operating against the flanks could have cut us off from the beaches and prevented the unloading of troops, supplies, and equipment. As it was, the Corps Beachhead Line was barely distant enough to prevent direct artillery fire on the beaches."
Major-General Lucien K. Truscott

Allied landing (LEFT)
US tanks stream into Anzio, 1944.

Amphibious landings (INSET)
Map shows Anzio landings.

The Great Escape

"The Germans were furious and the Gestapo took over the camp. In reprisal they picked forty-seven field grade flying officers, lined them up and shot them; then brought their ashes back into camp. This was the Gestapo method of discouraging escape attempts."

Lieutenant David Purner, Stalag Luft III, diary entry for April 1, 1944

Large numbers of prisoners of war were taken by both sides during World War II. Generally, their treatment was appalling. However, the Germans treated prisoners of the Western Allies well, and Allied officers made a sport of trying to escape. One camp, Stalag Luft III, for captured airmen, was the scene of two of the best-known escapes of the war.

The Germans treated prisoners of the Western Allies according to the Geneva Convention (1906). Enlisted men were paid to work, while officers were confined to POW camps. Soviet prisoners of the Germans did not fare so well. More than half died in captivity, and a similar proportion were deported as forced laborers to Germany. The Soviet Union and Japan had not signed the Geneva Convention. In their hands, hundreds of thousands of prisoners died. The Japanese were particularly brutal to the Chinese they captured. Western Allies also committed atrocities. Japanese prisoners were sometimes executed after capture. In 1945, German POWs were kept in open fields, where many died from starvation, dehydration, and exposure. Moreover, due to confusion at the end of WWII and the onset of the Cold War, British and American prisoners of war found themselves in Soviet labor camps, rather than being repatriated.

STALAG LUFT III

Opened in April 1942 at Sagan, Poland, Stalag Luft III was designed to be escape-proof. The first successful breakout occurred in October 1943, when three British airmen escaped through a tunnel whose entrance had been concealed under a wooden vaulting horse. All three made their way back to Britain. On the night of March 24, 1944, 76 men managed to

Allied escape (ABOVE)
Stalag Luft III was designed to be an entirely escape-proof prison.

A PRISONER OF WAR SPEAKS OUT

"Now I ask you my comrade, you who are far from your family and from your Fatherland? Do you remember still that this blood of your comrade does oblige you, also now in the prisoner of war camp, to stand for Germany as he did? I ask you, do you remember the day when you left your mother, father, wife, child or bride, brother and sister, when they were saying to you 'goodbye'? Do you think that they are trembling and praying for you and that they are longing for you? Do you remember that it is German blood running in your veins? Do you remember that day when you stood in formation and raised your hand to heaven to swear by God loyalty to the Führer and to the German people for life? It was our fate that we were taken prisoner and confined behind barbed wire. Disarmed and powerless we have to await the end of this war. But in spite of this we remain soldiers of our Führer, soldiers of that great army which is the best in the world."
Hans Niedermejer, speech in POW camp in Huntsville, Texas, September 1, 1943

Colditz Castle (BELOW)
Allied POWs who persistently escaped were sent to Colditz, near Leipzig.

escape through three tunnels in the "Great Escape." Only three reached safety. Fifty were caught and shot on Hitler's orders. Seventeen were returned to Stalag Luft III. Four were sent to Sachsenhausen concentration camp, where they succeeded in tunneling out under electric fences and doubled guards. Persistent escapees were sent to Colditz Castle near Leipzig, though several successful escapes were made from there too. There were other mass breakouts, but most escapees were recaptured. Many were executed or sent to concentration camps. However, breakouts succeeded in diverting enemy forces from the fronts. German prisoners escaped from camps in Canada and Wales, and were recaptured. Four Australian soldiers and 231 Japanese prisoners of war died in Australia in an uprising in Cowra, New South Wales.

Rome falls to the Allies

"Yesterday, on June 4, 1944, Rome fell to American and Allied troops. The first of the Axis capitals is now in our hands. One up and two to go."

President Roosevelt, "Fireside Chat", June 5, 1944

With the Gustav Line collapsing, Kesselring declared Rome to be an "open city" and evacuated his troops. US General Mark Clark made a dash for the city, entering it on June 5, 1944. It was a tremendous propaganda boost the day before D-Day. The capital of one of the Axis powers was now in Allied hands. However, Clark's dash on Rome was militarily a mistake.

Clark had missed the chance to encircle the German troops withdrawing from the Gustav Line. Instead they had been withdrawn in good order to another defensive line along the Arno river, 160 miles north of Rome. Churchill was adamant

Triumph in Rome (LEFT)
Allied tanks pass by the imposing bulk of the Coliseum, Rome, 1944.

Rome greets Allies (ABOVE)
Italian civilians watch as Allied tanks roll through the streets, 1944.

that the Allied forces should reach Yugoslavia and even Vienna before the Russians got there. He argued that Operation Dragoon, the Allied landings in the South of France that would follow the D-Day landings in Normandy, should be canceled and its men and materiel diverted to Italy. But even the British chiefs of staff doubted that General Harold Alexander's Eighth Army could reach the Alps by the end of the year, and the Americans were determined that Operation Dragoon should go ahead. Even so, the Allies overran the German defensive line along the Arno on August 13. By this time the Germans had had time to prepare a new line of defense called the Gothic Line. It ran 200 miles along the top of the mountain range from Pesaro on the eastern Adriatic coast to La Spezia on the western Gulf of Genoa. Work had begun reconnoitering defensive positions there almost a month before Axis troops were withdrawn from Sicily. German strong points were built astride the routes leading through the Apennines into the Po Valley. Every road and pass was blocked with German defenses.

CONSCRIPT LABOR

German engineers and conscripted Italian laborers built a series of positions to link the main strongholds in the mountains into one continuous defensive line, and they built a belt of obstacles ten miles deep along the whole front. As the Allies approached they faced miles of anti-tank ditches, 120,000 yards of wire entanglements, 2,376 machine-gun nests, and 479 anti-tank gun, mortar, and assault gun positions. However, the defenses were not quite finished. Only four of the thirty 7.5cm Panther tank gun turrets that the engineers had ordered were in place. But due to General Clark's ill-advised dash for Rome, Kesselring had managed to withdraw ten divisions to the Gothic Line. Ferocious fighting in northern Italy for another eight months meant that Vienna would fall to the Soviets.

The French Resistance

"Throughout France the Resistance had been of inestimable value in the campaign. Without their great assistance the liberation of France would have consumed a much longer time and meant greater losses to ourselves."

Dwight D. Eisenhower, Crusade in Europe *(1948)*

By June 1944, there were thought to be 100,000 members of the French Resistance—known as the *maquis* in rural areas. They published underground newspapers, spied for the Allies, sabotaged armaments factories, derailed trains, smuggled downed airmen out of the country, and attacked German soldiers. They played a significant part in the liberation of Paris, and their numbers had swelled to 400,000 by October of that year.

In the first two years since the occupation of France in 1940, most people kept faith with Marshal Pétain—seen as the "savior of France" during World War I—and supported his government in Vichy. Opposition to the government was carried out only by a tiny, uncoordinated minority. However, an underground press sprang up and their distribution networks became the core of the Resistance. In January 1942, General de Gaulle, who was still based in London, sent his emissary Jean Moulin to organize the maquis. In May 1943, Moulin formed the National Council of Resistance, but the following month he was captured by the Gestapo, tortured, and died while being taken to Germany. Nevertheless, the Resistance continued, aided by the Free French in London, Britain's clandestine Special Operations Executive set up by Churchill, and the RAF who parachuted in weapons and agents. Coded messages were broadcast to the maquis by the BBC. The Resistance responded via clandestine radio operators called *pianistes*. Due to German radio-detection equipment, each *pianiste* only lasted for around six months.

THE RESISTANCE IN ACTION

Early in the war, the Resistance started manufacturing explosives but found stealing dynamite from the Germans more effective. Blowing up military trains was their preferred means of attack because it led to fewer civilian casualties. In the run-up to D-Day in June 1944, the Resistance disrupted German communications and, after the D-Day landings, hampered German reinforcements getting to the front. The Resistance provided the Allies with a map and blueprint of the German defenses between Cherbourg and Le Havre, and details of German deployments. The Resistance fought alongside their Free French compatriots, and took over Paris before the Allies arrived.

The maquis (LEFT)
French Resistance fighters, known locally as maquisards, receive instructions before a raid, 1944.

French workers' warning (ABOVE)
A French Resistance poster painted by the American artist Ben Shahn, 1942.

WORK OF THE RESISTANCE

"In Brittany, southern France, and the area of the Loire and Paris, French Resistance forces greatly aided the pursuit to the Seine in August. Specifically, they supported the Third Army in Brittany and the Seventh US and First French Armies in the southern beachhead and the Rhône valley. In the advance to the Seine, the French Forces of the Interior helped protect the southern flank of the Third Army by interfering with enemy railroad and highway movements and enemy telecommunications, by developing open resistance on as wide a scale as possible, by providing tactical intelligence, by preserving installations of value to the Allied forces, and by mopping up bypassed enemy positions."
US Government Printing Office, Washington, D.C.

Operation Overlord

"What a plan! This vast operation is undoubtedly the most complicated and difficult that has ever taken place."

Winston Churchill, House of Commons, June 6, 1944

From the moment they had entered the war, the Soviets had been urging Britain to open a second front in northern France. The Americans were keen on a cross-Channel invasion. Finally Churchill, who was originally against it, could resist no longer. For political reasons, the commander of the invasion had to be an American. General Dwight D. Eisenhower was chosen.

Four British officers were in charge of actually running the landings: Eisenhower's deputy, Air Marshal Sir Arthur Tedder, at sea, Admiral Sir Bertram Ramsay, in the air, Air Chief Marshal Sir Trafford Leigh-Mallory and, on the ground, General Bernard Montgomery. Montgomery's first act was to throw away the invasion blueprint on which US planners had been working since 1942. The front was too narrow and the assault force too small. He increased the number of divisions landing on the beaches from three to five, and airborne divisions from one to three. Equal numbers of British and American troops would be landed but, as losses mounted, the British would be unable to sustain this commitment. Eventually, the war in Western Europe would become a predominantly American affair, so Eisenhower himself would take over command of the land forces once the beachhead was well established.

"THIS VAST OPERATION"

In the spring of 1944, southern England had become one huge parking lot for tanks, trucks, and airplanes. There were weapons and ammunition dumps in country lanes, and village pubs were full of soldiers from every part of the English-speaking world, along with Poles, Czechs, Hungarians, Free French, and Jews from all parts of Nazi-occupied Europe. More than six million people were mustered for the D-Day landings. At sea were 138 battleships, cruisers, and destroyers ready to

Taking the beaches (LEFT)
Allied forces land en masse at Omaha Bbach following the D-Day landings, France, 1944.

bombard the French coast. They were accompanied by 279 escorts, 287 minesweepers, 4 line-layers, 2 submarines, 495 motor boats, 310 landing ships, and 3,817 landing craft and barges for the initial assault. Another 410 landing craft would join them to transport more men and equipment ashore after the beachheads were secured. A further 423 ships, including tugs, would be involved in the construction of two prefabricated "Mulberry" harbors, which would be built in sections and towed across the Channel, then assembled at the landing beaches. The lesson of Dieppe had been learnt and there was little enthusiasm for taking an existing port. "Pluto", a pipeline to pump gasoline under the Channel, would have to be laid, along with telephone cables. Another 1,260 merchant ships would also be involved in supplying the landing force, making a total of over 7,400 vessels. Some 10,000 aircraft were also to be deployed in Operation Overlord. They would bomb key fortifications, drop paratroopers, tow gliders carrying airborne troops, attack enemy formations, and provide air superiority above the beaches.

OPERATION FORTITUDE

The British developed an elaborate deception, feeding the Germans disinformation that the invasion would take the direct route across the Straits of Dover. They invented the First US Army Group, a nonexistent army mustered in Kent. Radio traffic poured out of the area, and theatrical set-builders mocked up tanks and landing craft to fool German aerial reconnaissance. One badly wounded prisoner of war, a Panzer officer being returned to Germany, was led to believe that he had seen the First US Army Group—though the real vehicles were not in Kent at all but in Hampshire, ready for embarkation. Hitler became so convinced that the main attack would come in the Pas de Calais that he kept his Fifth Army there for seven weeks after the Allies had landed in Normandy.

D-Day

"This landing is part of the concerted United Nations' plan for the liberation of Europe, made in conjunction with our great Russian allies ... I call upon all who love freedom to stand with us ... Together we shall achieve victory."

General Dwight D. Eisenhower, broadcast, June 6, 1944

The landings were planned for June 5, 1944, and first-wave troops had already embarked on June 4 when a storm blew up. Eisenhower had no option but to postpone the invasion. But that night, the meteorologists thought that there might be a break in the weather the next day, and Eisenhower gave the order for the biggest invasion fleet ever assembled to set sail.

Huge waves of RAF heavy bombers flew across the Channel and blasted the coastal defenses of the Germans with 5,200 tons of bombs, and the railroads and bridges beyond the coast were taken out. That night, two American and one British airborne division were landed to secure the flanks of the invasion beaches and to destroy the coastal batteries. As dawn broke on June 6, the USAAF's medium-range bombers and

fighters took over, and later the navy continued the pounding of the emplacements behind the beaches. There were to be five invasion beaches—two US and three for the British and Canadians. Four of the beaches were taken quickly. But on Omaha beach the US First Division ran up against the battle-hardened German 352nd Infantry Division which had arrived from the Eastern Front the previous week. Against them were inexperienced men, because the US had a policy of selecting raw recruits, fearing that men who had seen action before would not run up a beach against enemy fire. With their amphibious tanks swamped, the Americans suffered 2,400 casualties at Omaha beach. Nevertheless, by the end of the day, all five divisions had established beachheads.

Into the fray (RIGHT)

View from an Allied landing craft as soldiers stream towards the beach, France, 1944.

COUNTERATTACK AT CAEN

Montgomery's plan called for the British to occupy Caen by the end of the first day. The British attacked and were repulsed in the only organized counterattack of the day. Only on July 11, five weeks after D-Day, was Caen finally taken. The cathedral and hospital alone remained standing. It is estimated that there were nearly 10,000 Allied casualties on D-Day—6,603 American, 2,700 British, and 946 Canadian—including 2,500 killed. The Germans lost between 4,000 and 9,000 men.

D-Day landings (BELOW)

Allied troops storm Omaha beach prior to a full-scale invasion of France, 1944.

A GERMAN SOLDIER ON D-DAY

"Around midnight on June 5–6 we received a telephone call raising security to level two. The deafening noise of aircraft engines confirmed that the invasion had begun. As our company assembled early that morning our area was carpet bombed. I was on my way to a meeting and found myself on the edge of the attack. Five soldiers of our company were buried in their foxholes and killed ..."
Alfred Mertens, 716 Regiment, Normandy

D-Day landings

"People of Western Europe: a landing was made this morning on the coast of France by troops of the Allied Expeditionary Force. "

General Dwight D. Eisenhower, broadcast, June 6, 1944

The D-Day landings were the largest amphibious landings ever staged. It was even bigger than the US planners had originally envisaged. After the commander-in-chief of the invasion, General Eisenhower, gave General Montgomery command of the landings, Montgomery tore up the US plans. He raised the number of amphibious troops landing from three divisions to five and the airborne divisions from one to three. US planners had originally mocked the idea of building the Mulberry harbors on the beaches, but they realized the impossibility of taking a port after the failure of the raid on Dieppe in August 1942. The landings were largely successful, except for the American assault on Omaha beach, which came up against experienced troops from the Eastern Front.

Canadians land in Normandy (BELOW)
By nightfall, Canadian troops had advanced farther inland than any other Allied force, D-Day, 1944.

Beach landing (ABOVE)
One of many amphibious landings by Allied troops.

Air support (RIGHT)
B-26 Marauder, en route to provide smokescreen cover during the D-Day landings, 1944.

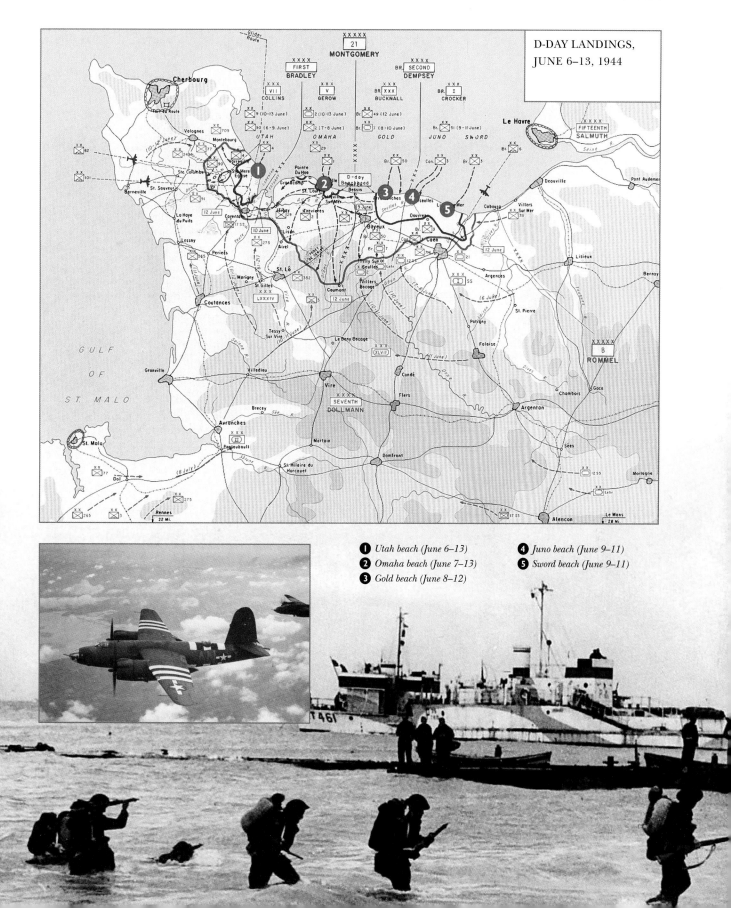

D-DAY LANDINGS, JUNE 6–13, 1944

❶ *Utah beach (June 6–13)*
❷ *Omaha beach (June 7–13)*
❸ *Gold beach (June 8–12)*
❹ *Juno beach (June 9–11)*
❺ *Sword beach (June 9–11)*

Battle of Normandy

"This is no longer a war here in Normandy. The enemy is superior in men and material. We are simply sent to our deaths with insufficient arms. Our Highest Command doesn't do anything to help us. No airplanes, insufficient ammunition for our artillery."

Corporal, Deutsche Kraus unit, decorated on the Eastern Front

Behind the beach defenses in Normandy was *bocage* country, where small fields are surrounded by drainage ditches and high earth banks, topped by thick hedges that arch over narrow sunken lanes. This is not good country for modern mechanized warfare. The cover it provides gives defenders an advantage. Fortunately one American soldier had studied the region when he visited it in 1912. His name was George S. Patton.

On June 12, 1944, the five American, British, and Canadian beachheads were finally joined, making an enclave 60 miles long and 15 miles deep. Then an American thrust across the Cotentin peninsula cut off Cherbourg. Another push created a 20-mile salient to the south. By June 18, there were 50,000 Allied men ashore, while German formations were being destroyed by planes flying from airstrips inside the beachheads. Then the worst storm for nearly 50 years hit. A dozen ships were sunk. The Mulberry harbor at Arromanches was badly damaged but remained usable; Omaha beach's harbor was destroyed. Suddenly the Allies were short of supplies and robbed of air cover. It was Rommel's chance to counterattack. But his forces were deployed for defense and were in no position to push the Allies back into the sea. By the end of the month the tonnage landing was back to pre-storm levels. Soon after, the port at Cherbourg became serviceable.

RAF BOMBS CAEN

Montgomery had kept up the pressure on Caen to keep the enemy off balance. German Panzers counterattacked, but came under withering air attack from the RAF's rocket-firing Typhoon fighter planes. Advancing through the bocage country, the Panzers were also vulnerable to the British Piat anti-tank weapon that could be fired at close range from behind the hedgerows. The five-day battle became so intense that the River Odon was dammed with bodies. It rained heavily throughout July and the fighting became—literally—bogged down. The RAF dropped 2,500 tons of bombs on Caen. After two days of fighting, the British took the northwestern part of the city at a cost of 3,500 casualties.

OPERATION GOODWOOD

A massive Allied attack was prepared on positions to the east and south of Caen. On the eve of the battle, Rommel was machine-gunned in his staff car by an RAF fighter. He took no further part in the fighting and committed suicide while convalescing after being implicated in a plot to kill Hitler. On the first day of Operation Goodwood, the British lost 1,500 men and 200 tanks, and failed to make a breakthrough. After 72 hours, the offensive was halted by a thunderstorm. Operation Goodwood finally convinced Hitler that there would be no attack from across the Straits of Dover. The Normandy landings were the real thing and he ordered the 250,000 men of his Fifteenth Army in the Pas de Calais into battle. Because of the devastation caused by Allied air strikes, the German took a month to reach Normandy. By that time one million Allied soldiers were ashore and the German Fifteenth Army proved to be too little too late.

Germans captured

Battle-weary German soldiers—among the first to be captured by the Allies on D-Day—wait to be sent to a POW camp in France, 1944.

BREAKOUT FROM THE BEACHHEAD

While the British kept the Germans occupied near Caen, 11,000 US troops were killed crossing the fields and marshes of western Normandy to take the smoldering ruins of St. Lô. This town stood at the head of a road that ran south to the Loire Valley. An Allied plan codenamed Operation Cobra was hatched to make a breakout there with a fast-moving tank column under General Patton.

Patton had landed on Utah beach on July 6 without even getting his feet wet, his previous transgressions in Sicily (when he'd accused two shell-shocked troops of cowardice) having been forgiven. From a well-camouflaged bivouac on the Cotentin Peninsula, he began to assemble his Third Army. Meanwhile, Hitler's Fifteenth Army was on its way to the east of the front and he felt it was safe to move seven of his divisions, including two Panzer divisions, to the west, bringing the number there up to 65. This strengthened the German line against any US breakout. It also lured the Germans into a deathtrap. On July 25, 3,000 USAAF bombers dropped 4,000 tons of high-explosive, fragmentation, and napalm bombs on a five-mile stretch of the German front to the west of St. Lô. The German commander General Bayerlein said that this raid turned the area into a *Mondlandshaft*—a moonscape. He estimated that 70 percent of the German troops in that section were put out of action, either dead, wounded, or driven mad by the bombing.

OUT OF THE BOCAGE

Patton's troops slowly moved forward through the bocage country—which the GIs had begun to call the "Gethsemane of the hedgerows." By July 27, Coutances was taken; by July 30, Avranches was taken and the German retreat had turned into a rout. Within 24 hours, Patton pushed three divisions through the five-mile gap that had opened at Avranches. His men were now out of the bocage country and onto the open roads of Brittany.

Closing the Falaise Gap

"I don't care for anything. Two of my brothers were sacrificed at
Stalingrad and it was quite useless, and here we have the same movie."

German infantryman, Normandy

Montgomery was making slow progress in the east of
Normandy in the summer of 1944, and turned his
troops to the south, while the Canadians advanced on Falaise.
General Omar Bradley sent Patton and his Third Army on a
long sweep south, then east, to encircle the Germans. Hitler
saw the danger too late. His army in Normandy would be
trapped in a pocket at Falaise and destroyed.

THE FALAISE POCKET

Hitler planned a counterattack against the bottleneck at
Avranches, intending to close the gap there and cut off
Patton's supply lines. But characteristically Hitler was 800 miles
away in his headquarters, the Wolf's Lair, in East Prussia and
his troops walked into a trap. His commanders on the ground
knew that the battle for Normandy was lost and they should
make an orderly retreat across the Seine. As the German
Fifteenth Army advanced from the Pas de Calais, Allied
bombers cut off its retreat by destroying the remaining bridges
along the Seine. Meanwhile, Patton was making quick time
across the open roads of northwest France, taking Le Mans on
August 8. To the north, five Panzer and two infantry divisions
on their way to Avranches ran into a single American division
at Mortain. But the Americans held them. Powerful US
formations struck back through Vire, while the British pushed
from the north against Condé and Patton turned north. The
Germans were now caught in a small pocket between Mortain
and Falaise, where the Allied air forces relentlessly bombed
and strafed them. By August 14, the only way out for the
Germans was through an 18-mile gap between the Canadians
at Falaise and Patton's Third Army. Patton wanted to drive on
to Falaise and close the gap but his speeding army had lost its
coherence and Bradley ordered him to stop.

Refused permission by Hitler to retreat, German units were
being cut down by the French Resistance or were surrendering

T.C. POST
100 yds

Falaise aftermath (RIGHT)
*Exhausted German prisoners are driven
through the debris at Falaise, 1944.*

158

wholesale to Allied forces. Rommel's replacement, Field Marshal Gunther von Kluge, got lost in the confusion. After he reappeared, he was relieved of his command and committed suicide. By August 18, the Falaise gap was squeezed to six miles and Allied air attacks on it were so relentless that any attempt to get through resulted in almost certain death. The gap was sealed on August 20. Some 10,000 Germans were killed in six days in the Falaise Gap and 50,000 prisoners were taken. Of the thousands who escaped, many more were killed before

they reached the Seine. Thousands more who were cut off elsewhere gave themselves up. Two Panzer divisions and eight infantry divisions were captured almost entirely. In all, German casualties in Normandy amounted to 400,000 men, half of whom were captured. The Allied casualties totaled 209,672 men, of whom 36,976 were killed. The Germans also lost 1,300 tanks, 1,500 guns, and 20,000 vehicles. What remained of the German Army in western Europe fled headlong for the German border.

German retreat (RIGHT)
US troops shell German forces near Carentan, France, 1944.

CARNAGE ON THE BATTLEFIELD

"The battlefield at Falaise was unquestionably one of the greatest killing grounds of any of the war areas. Roads, highways and fields were so choked with destroyed equipment and with dead men and animals that passage through the area was extremely difficult. Forty-eight hours after the closing of the gap, I was conducted through on foot, to encounter a scene that could be described only by Dante. It was quite literally possible to walk for hundreds of yards at a time, stepping on nothing but dead and decaying flesh."
General Dwight D. Eisenhower

Operation Dragoon

"The invasion is nothing more than an ingenious, strategic coup by Hitler. The Allies have been lured into France so they are no longer out of reach as they were when they were in England. Now that we have them within reach, our troops will destroy them."

Joseph Goebbels, Nazi propaganda minister.

Even Hitler said it was the worst day of his life when, on August 15, 1944, the Allies began amphibious landings on the Côte d'Azur. Originally designated Operation Anvil, the name had been changed to Dragoon by Churchill, who favored an attack in the Balkans and felt he had been dragooned into the attack on the South of France by the Americans.

LANDINGS IN THE SOUTH OF FRANCE

Early on the morning of August 15, Allied planes dropped dummy parachutists west of the port of Toulon to confuse the enemy, while Allied craft towed radar-reflecting balloons to make it appear that a huge naval force was arriving. To the east the "Devil's Brigade," a Special Services unit of Americans and Canadians, landed on the Iles d'Hyères. A French commando team cut off the road to Toulon, while another team under the movie star Douglas Fairbanks, Jr., then a lieutenant-commander in the US Navy, landed near Cannes. They were captured by the Germans but freed within 24 hours by the Allied invasion. At 04:30 hours, the first of 396 Dakota bombers flying from airfields in Italy was over the drop zone around Le Muy, ten miles inland. A low-lying fog convinced the paratroopers they were landing in the sea, and some jettisoned heavy equipment and their weapons. The planes were scattered. At 09:20 hours, the first wave of gliders arrived. Two had been lost on the way. One disintegrated, scattering men and equipment across the sea. No-one survived. Another glider ditched safely near an Allied ship. The remaining 71 gliders reached the landing zone, but trees there caused a huge loss of life as the gliders crashed into them.

AMPHIBIOUS LANDINGS

Coastal defenses were pounded by Allied naval gunfire. Minesweepers went in to clear a path close to shore. Then radio-controlled boats packed with explosives blasted a route to the beaches. They were followed by landing craft firing waves of rockets. Two divisions got ashore with little trouble, but a third ran into an unexpected minefield and withering German fire that the naval gunfire could not suppress. More divisions were diverted further down the beach. Another 332 gliders landed at dusk. That night some 9,000 airborne Allied troops were in position, along with 221 jeeps and 213 artillery pieces, though 434 men had been killed and 292 injured. The following evening forward elements of the amphibious force joined up with the airborne force. The beachhead had been consolidated and by midnight on August 17 more than 86,500 troops, 12,500 vehicles, and 46,100 tons of supplies had been landed. The Luftwaffe made only a token response, then withdrew from southern France, leaving the skies to the USAAF, which bombed bridges and strafed road and rail traffic to devastating effect. Meanwhile, the French Resistance harassed Panzers moving north toward Normandy. In the meantime Bletchley Park decoded a message from General Johannes von Blaskowitz ordering a withdrawal. The Seventh Army under Lieutenant-General Alexander M. "Sandy" Patch gave chase, while the airborne infantry liberated Cannes and Nice, and the Free French II Corps headed for Toulon and Marseilles.

Reaching the South of France (RIGHT)
US troops disembark from a naval landing craft at Toulon, France, 1944.

Fighting for freedom (RIGHT)
*A French Resistance fighter and a US
soldier crouch by an automobile.*

Allied forces advance

"The quicker we clean up this Goddamned mess, the quicker we can take a little jaunt against the ... Japs and clean out their nest, too."

General George S. Patton

After General Patton broke out of the Normandy beachhead at the head of his Third Army at the end of July 1944, Hitler fell into the Allied trap. He sent in the reserves he had been holding back in the Pas de Calais, thinking the main invasion would come there. Hitler's reserve troops found themselves encircled with other German troops retreating from the beaches and were destroyed by Allied bombing. Then the Allies raced for the German border. It seemed that the war was all but over, but it wasn't. There was still much hard fighting to be done during the next ten months, in the Ardennes, at Arnhem, and in Germany itself, all the way to Berlin.

The Allies advance
Map shows sweep of Allied troops in fall 1944, liberating Occupied France and the Low Countries and heading toward Germany.

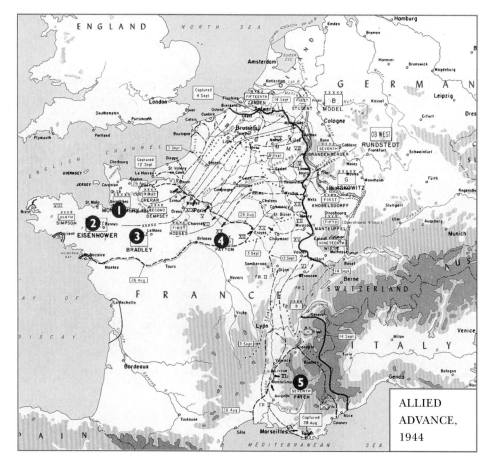

❶ *Montgomery*
❷ *Eisenhower*
❸ *Bradley*
❹ *Patton*
❺ *Patch*

1 *Operation Market Garden*
2 *Model (German)*
3 *Rundstadt (German)*
4 *Montgomery (Allied)*
5 *Eisenhower (Allied)*
6 *Bradley (Allied)*
7 *Patton (Alllied)*

Allied troops advance
US paratroopers move inland,
France, 1944.

THE ALLIES
ADVANCE, FALL
1944

Paris falls to the Allies

"Paris must not fall into enemy hands, but, if it does, he must find nothing but ruins."

Adolf Hitler

With the Falaise Gap closed, Patton's Third Army raced eastward, crossing the Seine on August 19, 1944. The British followed on August 25. Eisenhower then decided the Allies would bypass Paris to avoid the destruction and loss of life that a battle for the city would entail. Hitler had intended to turn Paris into a fortress but, given the hopelessness of the position, ordered it to be burned down.

For over four years, the Parisians had suffered the humiliation of occupation. Every day for 1,500 days, German troops had marched down the Champs Elysées. On August 10, 1944, French railroad men called a strike. Electricity and gas supplies became sporadic and the Métro stopped running. On August 13, the Germans started disarming the city's 20,000 gendarmes, who promptly joined the strike. Soon sporadic gunfire was heard. The SS reacted by machine-gunning 35 French youths. All significant buildings were mined by the Germans ready for demolition, but the city's commandant Lieutenant-General Dietrich von Choltitz stayed his hand. On August 19, 2,000 striking policemen seized the Préfecture de Police. They hoisted the Tricolor and sang the *Marseillaise*, and when German tanks appeared in the Boulevard de Palais they were fired upon. The Palais de Justice and the Hôtel de Ville were seized by the French. The revolutionary cry "*aux barricades*" went up. Cobblestones were torn up and hundreds of barricades, made from overturned vehicles and felled trees, were manned by Parisians in makeshift uniforms. By August 22, there was open warfare on the streets. By the next night, the Grand Palais was on fire, hit by an incendiary round, and 500 Parisians were dead.

"IS PARIS BURNING?"

The Resistance begged for help. Eisenhower ordered General Omar Bradley to take the city. Meanwhile, German tanks roamed the streets, machine-guns blazing. However, aside from the Germans' central stronghold, the city was almost entirely in the hands of the Resistance. For political reasons, Eisenhower ordered that the first unit into Paris was to be the Second Free French Armored Division under Major-General Philippe Leclerc. At 21:22 hours on August 24, six Free French half-tracks and three tanks arrived at the Hôtel de Ville. Their presence was announced by the ringing of church bells. When Hitler heard of this, he asked: "Is Paris burning?" The following morning Leclerc's main force swept into the city from the southwest, while the US Fourth Infantry liberated the eastern section. By 10:00 hours the next day, only a few pockets of German resistance remained and von Choltitz signed documents surrendering the city to Leclerc. The next day, the Free French leader General Charles de Gaulle made a triumphal entry to the city.

Captured in Paris (LEFT)
German prisoners are marched away by a wounded French trooper, Arc de Triomphe, Paris, 1944.

Liberation of France (ABOVE)
Allied tanks sweep through the streets of Paris following the liberation of the city, 1944.

Warsaw destroyed

"I reached Marszalowska Street without any problem, but no further, for the shooting from the direction of the Saski Park is furious ... The street has a sinister look: glass, broken bricks and wires litter it ... I am gripped by fear, again."

Diary of Teresa Wilska Bozenka, August 3, 1944

At the end of July 1944, Warsaw was in its fifth year of German occupation. On the Eastern Front, the Germans were in full retreat after the Red Army's spring offensive. The liberation of Poland's capital seemed imminent. However, when the Red Army reached the Vistula river near Warsaw, it stopped. The city had already suffered so much. Now it faced complete destruction.

As they approached the city, the Soviets encouraged the Warsaw underground—the Home Army numbering around 50,000—to revolt against the German garrison. Loyal to the Polish government-in-exile in London, it was eager to do so before the Soviets entered the city, because Moscow was already preparing its own Communist-led government to take over in Poland. The Home Army attacked the garrison on August 1 and within three days had taken over most of the city. But the Germans sent reinforcements unhindered by the Russians. For the next 63 days Warsaw was pounded by bombs and shells.

THE CITY DESTROYED

The Red Army did nothing. Stalin refused the Western Allies permission to use Soviet airfields to fly supplies into the beleaguered Poles, and even ordered the disarmament of Home Army reinforcements trying to infiltrate the city. Without ammunition and food, the Home Army was forced to surrender to the Germans on October 2. Warsaw's population was deported to Germany and the city destroyed. When the Soviets finally forced the Germans out of Poland, the way was open for them to install their own pro-Soviet regime on January 1, 1945. The Soviets' collusion in the destruction of Warsaw was particularly embarrassing for the British, who had gone to war over the German invasion of Poland in 1939. "Such was their liberation of Poland," said Churchill, "where they now rule. But this cannot be the end of the story."

Civilian prisoners (ABOVE)
German soldiers march Jewish civilians out of the ruins of the Warsaw ghetto, Poland, 1944.

DESPERATE TIMES IN WARSAW

"About half the population have been wounded or killed. Almost every soldier, if not killed, has received a wound of some sort. The population shelter in cellars, which often become collective graves ... In the large concentration camp on the city's outskirts there are tens of thousands of Polish people who are starving to death ... All Polish military prisoners who fall into German hands are murdered."
John War, escaped POW with the Home Army, September 4, 1944

A city in ruins (BELOW)
*The remnants of the historic Square
of the Three Crosses, Warsaw, 1944.*

Arnhem

"The bullets hitting the water looked like a hailstorm, kicking up little spouts of water. When we reached about the halfway point, then the mortar and artillery fire started falling. And when a boat was hit with an artillery shell or a mortar shell, it just disintegrated, and everybody was lost."

Moffat Buriss, 82nd Airborne Division

On September 1, 1944, Montgomery relinquished overall command of the Allied land forces to Eisenhower. Then, while US forces dashed across France, Montgomery and the British forces headed north toward Belgium and the V-1 and V-2 sites. Normally a cautious man, Montgomery proposed a bold move that, if successful, would put his Second Army into the German industrial heartland before the winter.

The idea was to use airborne troops to seize eight bridges on the road from Eindhoven to Arnhem, then drive the Second Army down the road, through the German border defenses,

Crash landing (RIGHT)
An Allied paratrooper lands awkwardly during Operation Market Garden, the Netherlands, 1944.

Taking to the air (INSET)
RAF photographic reconnaissance Spitfire plane over the Netherlands, 1944.

and into the Ruhr. The airborne part of the plan was called Operation Market, the armored part Operation Garden. Together they would be known as Operation Market Garden. Montgomery persuaded Eisenhower that the fleeing German Army was so disorganized that it would not be able to stage effective resistance. American airdrops by the 101st and 82nd Airborne Divisions on September 17, 1944, took the bridges at Eindhoven and Nijmegen, and the British 30th Corps began its 64-mile dash from the Meuse-Escaut Canal. However, the British

paratroopers and gliders landed too far from the bridges they planned to seize. By the time they arrived, the Germans had been alerted and the British paratroopers managed to capture only the north end of one of the bridges.

COUNTERATTACK

Bad weather and German assaults on the 30th Corps, who were attacking up a single road, one-tank wide, denied the advance guard any relief. The enclave held by the British airborne troopers was gradually reduced. They had few anti-tank weapons to defend themselves from the Panzers that staged a counterattack. On September 25, the British parachute division was ordered to pull back to the area held by the 30th Corps across a river in range of German artillery. Some 2,500 British troops made the crossing, but they left behind nearly 1,500 dead and more than 6,500 prisoners, many badly wounded.

AIRBORNE TROOPS AT ARNHEM

"My first reaction was one of enormous enthusiasm and excitement, because this was the first time that anyone on our side had contemplated the proper strategic use of airborne forces en masse … I think everyone at that stage felt totally confident they would win. Certainly the flight over from England was absolutely beautiful. There was an absolute mass, an armada as far as the eye could see, in both directions, and about twenty planes wide, the most extraordinary sight I've ever seen … We really had nothing we could do to them, and they drove up and down the street, firing high explosive into the side of the building, to create the gap, and then firing smoke shells through that. The phosphorus from the smoke shells burned us out. By about eight o'clock, on Wednesday evening, the fires got out of control and of course we had by this time about three hundred wounded in the cellars."

Major Tony Hibbert, First Parachute Brigade

Greece and the Balkans

"My mission was simply to find out who was killing the most Germans and suggest means by which we could help them to kill more."

Diplomat Fitzroy MacLean, Eastern Approaches *(1980)*

Greece had suffered badly during World War II. There had been a famine in 1941 because the Germans and Italians had denied supplies to the population, and by a blockade which had been imposed by the British. This was lifted the following year when it became clear that it was affecting the Greek people and not their occupiers. After the fall of Crete in May 1941, King George II of Greece and the Greek armed forces escaped. The Greek Army and Navy fought alongside the British in North Africa, while King George headed for the US, where he addressed a joint session of Congress and appealed for aid. The American people responded by sending food.

GREEK RESISTANCE

Partisans took to the Greek hills and in November 1942 British and Greek soldiers parachuted into Greece to direct the resistance. But there was conflict been Communist and anti-Communist groups. There was a similar falling out between royalist and republican factions in the military. Rifts were only healed when the new Greek government-in-exile under the centrist George Papandreou was formed. The partisans then did an effective job of harassing the German and Italian occupiers, who responded by destroying 879 villages and killing more that 400,000 Greeks, mainly civilians. Over 67,000 Greek Jews were sent to Auschwitz, 43,000 from Thessaloniki alone. Few survived. However, the people of Athens and the partisans made many selfless efforts to prevent their deportation.

THE LIBERATION OF GREECE

When Italy surrendered, the Germans disarmed its soldiers in Greece and 5,000 were massacred on the island of Cephalonia. But by August 1944, with the Red Army sweeping through Romania into the Balkans, the Germans

in Greece risked being cut off and withdrew to the sound of bells and cheering crowds waving Greek flags. The British landed in Patras in the Gulf of Corinth on October 4, 1944 and, meeting little opposition, pushed on toward Athens. On October 14, 1944, Colonel Earl Jellicoe and a small group of British soldiers—accompanied by a swelling band of Greek partisans—made their way down 28 miles of blown-up roads from the small airfield at Megara, which they had captured a few days before, into the Greek capital, Athens. The city was bedecked with banners and flowers, and was full of cheering crowds. But the suffering of the Greek people did not end with liberation. Food shortages continued with hyperinflation. Then the country was plunged into a civil war.

PARTISAN RESISTANCE IN YUGOSLAVIA

In Yugoslavia, a country formed after World War I from Balkan provinces of the Austro-Hungarian Empire, there were mixed feelings about the German invasion in April 1941. In Croatia, the right-wing Ustasa (Croatian fascists), welcomed it and set up their own independent state. The royalist Chetniks, remnants of the Yugoslav army, aimed to wait for the Allies to arrive, then restore the monarchy. Then there were the Communist partisans.

The Communists, under party leader Josip Broz Tito (1892–1980), did nothing to antagonize the Germans until Germany turned on the Soviet Union in June 1941. Then the Communists began small-scale sabotage. In September 1941, they occupied the Serbian town of Uzice and proclaimed a republic. This alienated the Chetniks who remained loyal to King Peter II. The two groups also fell out over the atrocities committed by the Germans in reprisal for acts of resistance. The Chetniks wished to avoid provoking German reprisals, while Tito believed that they helped drive people to join his Communist partisans. Growing in strength, Tito began calling his followers the People's Liberation Army (PLA) and, in November 1942, set up what would become a provisional government. Fearful that the Allies might launch an invasion through the Balkans, the Germans and Italians mounted seven major offensives against the partisans.

ALLIED SUPPORT

In 1943, Churchill sent the diplomat and SAS officer Fitzroy MacLean to Yugoslavia to find out what was going on. He contacted Tito. The Allies then shifted their support from the Chetniks to Tito's partisans, supplying them with arms and leaving the Chetniks, on occasions, to fight alongside the German and Italians against their Communist rivals. By 1944, the PLA had grown to some 300,000 men and was holding down almost 40 Axis divisions, drawing them away from other fronts. In October 1944, the PLA joined the Red Army in the liberation of Belgrade. The partisans then attacked and killed the Chetniks. On March 1, 1945, the PLA became the Yugoslav People's Army and Tito established a Communist state. However, during the ensuing Cold War between the Soviet Bloc and the West, Yugoslavia remained neutral.

Striking back
Greek resistance fighters fire at a German-held police station during a civil uprising in Athens, Greece, 1944.

MacArthur returns

"Will the American and the Filipino armies spare us? The fact that they shoot at us every day and kill almost anything they encounter leads me to believe that they have no desire to spare us. I certainly want to live. I cannot die without knowing the situation in the world."

Diary of Commander Tadakazu Yoshioka,
26th Air Flotilla, Luzon, June 8

On leaving the Philippines in March 1942, General Douglas MacArthur had vowed famously: "I will return." On October 21, 1944, he fulfilled his promise, wading ashore on the central island of Leyte, wearing his famous sunglasses and battered service cap. There was little opposition to the Americans. The Japanese had been expecting an attack on the most southerly island, Mindanao.

In mid-September, MacArthur's forces from New Guinea had first seized Morotai, the most northeasterly island of the Moluccas, while Admiral Chester Nimitz's fleet had landed troops on the Palau Islands to the east. Bypassing Mindanao, US forces seized offshore islands in Leyte Gulf on October 17 and 18. On October 20 they landed four divisions on the east coast of Leyte itself. In response, Admiral Jisaburo Ozawa sailed south from Japanese waters with four aircraft carriers transporting 106 planes to be flown by trained kamikaze pilots. Meanwhile, two battleships, one heavy cruiser, and four destroyers under Vice-Admiral Nishimura Teiji would enter the Gulf of Leyte from the southwest, while five battleships, twelve cruisers, and fifteen destroyers under Vice-Admiral Kurita Takeo would enter from the north. However, on the way two of Takeo's cruisers were torpedoed by US submarines and the *Musashi*, one of Japan's mightiest battleships, was sunk in an air attack.

NO LONGER A THREAT

As the commander of the US Third Fleet, Admiral William Halsey had headed north toward Ozawa's fleet, while Takeo

sailed unopposed through the San Bernardino Strait. But Teiji's fleet was spotted in the Surigao Strait and almost annihilated. Finding himself alone in Leyte Gulf, Takeo turned back. Meanwhile, Halsey had destroyed all four of Ozawa's carriers, together with a light cruiser and two destroyers. After the Battle of Leyte Gulf, the Japanese Navy was no longer a threat, but the Americans took another two months to clear Leyte against a defense that cost the Japanese 75,000 men. US forces landed on Luzon island on January 9, 1945. The Philippines capital, Manila, fell to the Americans on March 3 but Japanese resistance continued in the mountains until June. Meanwhile, an American division landed on Mindanao on March 10. Japanese resistance in the Philippines ended on June 18. The Philippines were declared liberated on July 5, though old Japanese soldiers were still being found in the jungle 30 years later.

MacArthur returns (RIGHT)
General Douglas MacArthur makes his promised return to the Philippines, coming ashore at Luzon, 1944.

Americans on Leyte Island (INSET)
Allied soldiers build sandbag piers to the ramps to speed up unloading operations, the Philippines, 1944.

The Ardennes

"Soldiers of the west front. Your great hour has arrived. Large attacking armies have started against the Anglo-Americans. I do not have to tell you anything more than that. You feel it yourselves. We gamble everything."

Message to the troops from Field Marshal von Rundstedt, December 16, 1944

With Germany retreating on all fronts, even Hitler realized that victory by force of arms was no longer within his grasp. But the failure of Operation Market Garden emboldened him. A decisive victory in the west might force the Allies to the negotiating table. He might even persuade them to join him and take on the Soviet Union.

On September 16, 1944, while listening to a situation report on the Western Front, Hitler suddenly announced: "I shall go on the offensive … out of the Ardennes, with the objective, Antwerp." An attack through the Ardennes had worked in 1940. If successful, it would sever the American supply lines and cut off the British in Belgium and Holland. When Field Marshal Gerd von Rundstedt, recently reinstated as German commander in the west, heard about the plan he was horrified. In 1940, he had sent 2,500 tanks into France. Now, against far superior forces, Hitler planned to send just 1,420 tanks, which would have to capture American gasoline on the way since the Germans had run out. Moreover, the Germans had enjoyed air superiority in 1940, but now they had lost it. Back then, Germany had overwhelming numbers of men—now the US did. Running true to form, Hitler ignored his most experienced general. However, he was persuaded to delay the attack until December 16 to muster enough troops for the offensive. Although ill and exhausted, Hitler switched his headquarters to the Eagle's Lair in the Rhineland so as to direct the battle personally. Those closest to him noted that he was getting increasingly out of touch with reality.

BEHIND ALLIED LINES

In November, while German preparations were underway, the Allies breached the Siegfried Line and took Aachen, the first German town to fall to the Allies. Allied army intelligence had ruled out a German offensive in the Ardennes, despite the lesson of 1940. There were just four US divisions in the area—two that had just been pulled out of the line after heavy fighting and two that had never seen action before. They were about to be hit by 3 German armies, 25 divisions in all, 11 of them armored. To blunt any counteroffensive, Hitler sent behind enemy lines some English-speaking German troops under SS Colonel Otto Skorzeny, who had led the daring raid to rescue Mussolini from prison in 1943. Carrying American weapons and wearing American uniforms, they would disrupt Allied forces by misdirecting traffic and switching signposts.

German counteroffensive (INSET)
A German soldier carries ammunition boxes through recaptured territory, Belgium, 1944.

Tanks to Ardennes (BELOW)
German troops and tanks head for the Ardennes, Belgium, 1944.

The Battle of the Bulge

"The present situation is to be regarded as one of opportunity for us and not disaster.
There will be only cheerful faces at this conference table."

General Eisenhower, Verdun, December 19, 1944

Eisenhower was taken completely by surprise to learn that 2,000 guns opened up in the Ardennes at 05:35 hours on December 16. The weather was bad and the Allied air forces were grounded. The Germans quickly developed a salient 50 miles deep into the American lines. Churchill quickly dismissed the attack as "The Battle of the Bulge." Skorzeny's troops fooled no one and most of them faced the firing squad as spies, since they were caught wearing American uniforms. The Sixth SS Panzer Army made significant gains, which they could not exploit due to lack of fuel. The Fifth Panzer Army reaching Celles, six miles short of the River Meuse, where it was halted when the weather cleared and Allied air forces took to the skies again. The Fifth Panzers' supply route ran through the town of Bastogne, which was held by the 101st Airborne division under Brigadier-General Anthony McAuliffe. When asked to surrender, he replied famously: "Nuts." The 101st held out for six days, supplied from the air. Meanwhile, Patton's Third Army turned north to attack the left flank of the Germans, while the newly promoted Field Marshal Montgomery attacked the right flank.

CRUSHING DEFEAT

On December 22, von Rundstedt was refused permission by Hitler to withdraw. On Christmas Day, the Sixth Panzers suffered a crushing defeat and the following day Bastogne was relieved, at a cost of 3,900 American and 12,000 German dead in total. The Americans lost 150 tanks in the action, the Germans 450. Hitler had no choice but to withdraw now because German atrocities had inspired the US troops to fight with renewed determination. By early January 1945, the German front line was almost back where it had been before the "Battle of the Bulge". The Germans had lost 100,000 men, the Americans 81,000, and the British, who played only a minor part in the action, 1,400. Both sides had lost an enormous amount of tanks and equipment. The relentless Allied bombing of their cities meant the Germans could not replace their equipment. The Allies could.

ATROCITIES

Leading the German advance guard was General Jochen Peiper. At Honsfeld, his men shot 19 GIs and robbed their dead bodies. At an airfield near Bullingen, Peiper forced captured Americans to refuel his tanks. Afterwards, he shot them. Eight more Allied prisoners of war were killed at Ligneuville. One hundred American prisoners were machine-gunned in Malmédy. Twenty Americans who miraculously escaped hid in a café. It was set on fire and they were machine-gunned when they ran out. Hitler thought that news of these massacres would demoralize the American troops. In fact, it gave them the greatest incentive to fight back.

A CONDEMNED MAN WRITES HOME

"I broke the laws of the Geneva convention while carrying out orders and we will be shot according to the law. With this letter I say goodbye to you and to our dear parents. The shots that will extinguish the flame of my life will destroy a happy marriage. But we don't want to be angry with fate and neither leave room for hate. The men who are performing my execution are fighting without hate for a better, happier Europe. Therefore, I ask you, may you also be without hate, try to understand. I have understood. My verdict may be very hard, but it is correct according to the laws of Geneva."
Last letter to his wife from German prisoner Gorlich, condemned after the massacre of American troops at Malmédy, December 30, 1944

Germans advance (LEFT)
Weary German troops pass burning US vehicles during their push to the Ardennes, 1944.

US troops fight back (ABOVE)
News of German atrocities inspired American soldiers to redouble efforts in the Battle of the Bulge, 1944.

The Red Cross

"No relief action of any sort by the Red Cross in Germany or the occupied territories could have been undertaken without the approval of the authorities … Conforming to the letter, if not to the spirit of the Geneva Conventions … the Nazi government refused to allow any intervention on the part of the Red Cross in the concentration camps."

Roger Du Pasquier, International Committee of the Red Cross

Under the 1929 Geneva Convention, the International Committee of the Red Cross (ICRC) was charged with visiting and monitoring prisoner-of-war camps, organizing relief assistance for civilian populations, and administering the exchange of messages regarding prisoners and missing persons. But despite its best efforts to discharge these duties, the ICRC was severely criticized after the war was over.

DISTRIBUTION OF AID

By the end of the war, 179 ICRC delegates had conducted 12,750 visits to POW camps in 41 countries. In enormously difficult circumstances, the ICRC had supervised the distribution of humanitarian aid in the form of Red Cross food parcels, sent by national organizations, to prisoners of war and those British subjects cut off on the Channel Islands. Meanwhile, the 3,000 staff of the ICRC's Central Information Agency on Prisoners-of-War had built up an index of 45 million cards, with information on prisoners, and had exchanged 120 million messages. However, neither the Soviet Union nor Japan had signed the 1929 Geneva Conventions so the ICRC was denied access to POW camps there. Until November 1943, the ICRC was also refused permission to monitor the treatment of detainees in Nazi concentration camps, and eventually abandoned attempts to apply pressure on the Nazis to avoid jeopardizing its work with POWs. Although it received reliable information about the extermination camps and the mass murder of European Jews, there was little it could do about it.

However, after November 1943 the ICRC did receive from the Nazis permission to send parcels to Nazi concentration-camp detainees, when it knew their names and locations. Since receipts for these parcels were often signed by other inmates, the ICRC managed to register the identities of about 105,000 detainees in the concentration camps and delivered some 1.1 million parcels, mainly to Dachau, Buchenwald, Ravensbrück, and Sachsenhausen. Then on March 12, 1945, the ICRC president, Jacob Burckhardt, received permission to visit the concentration camps, provided their delegates stayed in the camps until the end of the war. Ten delegates volunteered. One of them, Louis Haefliger, prevented the Germans' attempt to evict POWs and destroy Mauthausen camp by alerting advancing US troops, saving the lives of about 60,000 inmates.

ICRC in Europe (BELOW)
Red Cross nurses with British forces, France.

Red Cross registers prisoner identities (BELOW)
*Allied POWs in Walzburg Castle concentration camp
receive Red Cross parcels, Bavaria, 1944.*

CONTENTS OF A BRITISH RED CROSS PARCEL

1/4 lb packet of tea
tin of cocoa powder
bar of milk or plain
chocolate
tinned pudding
tin of meat roll
tin of processed cheese
tin of condensed milk
tin of dried eggs
tin of sardines or
herrings

tin of preserve
tin of margarine
tin of sugar
tin of vegetables
tin of biscuits
bar of soap
tin of 50 cigarettes
or tobacco (sent
separately)

Counterattack in Burma

"Extract digit Japs gone."

Sign painted on the roof of Rangoon jail by POWs, May 1, 1945

Despite Japanese reverses in the Pacific, in early 1944, General Renya Mutagachi—"the victor of Singapore," now commander of the Japanese forces in Burma—received orders to take Assam. The aim was to halt the British preparations for a counterattack in Burma, then march across northern India and install a sympathetic government in Delhi under the Nazi-trained Indian nationalist Subhas Chandra Bose. It was an empty dream.

The British had already developed new tactics to deal with the Japanese. Instead of falling back in the face of an enemy advance, they set up well-defended enclaves that could be supplied by air. In January 1944, a Japanese counterattack in Arakan on the northwestern coast surrounded an Indian division, but the attackers found themselves crushed between the encircled Indians and the relieving force. The Japanese then made a thrust toward the British base at Imphal, cutting off the outpost at Kohima. But the British now had superiority in tanks and in the air, and Indian reinforcements, who remained loyal to the British, were moved up from Arakan. Despite hand-to-hand fighting, the British forces resisted numerous assaults. Without supplies, the Japanese found themselves starving in the jungle and were eventually forced to withdraw. They lost 30,500 dead, including 8,400 from disease, and 30,000 wounded. The British and Indian forces suffered 17,587 casualties. The Japanese were now a spent force in Burma, but continued fighting as they were pushed back throughout the rest of the war. The capital, Rangoon, fell to the Allies on May 1. Although he succeeded in raising the Indian tricolor on Indian soil for the first time, Subhas Chandra Bose's dream of liberating India from British rule had failed. He flew back to Singapore and was never heard of again.

NORTHERN BURMA

While the British were defending Imphal in the south, General Stilwell's forces and the Chindits were advancing in northern Burma in an attempt to reopen the Burma Road. On May 17, "Merril's Marauders" (Stilwell's Chinese division) took Myitkyina airfield. The Chindits took Mogaung on June 26, and Merril's

Marauders took Myitkyina itself on August 3. With him were US engineers building a new "Stilwell Road," which linked up with the old Burma Road at Lashio in February 1945. The whole road from Burma to China was only cleared in June 1945, when the Japanese were near defeat.

Keeping watch (RIGHT)
Allied soldiers observe Japanese troop movements, Burma, 1944.

Captured sniper (BELOW)
A British soldier escorts a captured Japanese sniper, Burma, 1944.

A JAPANESE SOLDIER IN BURMA

"There were only 700 Japanese soldiers there to defend the town without any aid, while four divisions of Allies with air-support and modern equipment violently attacked the small base town about two square kilometers. Due to the extreme shortage of ammunition and food, battle casualties and other losses on our side mounted. In order to survive, I had to sip dew-drops from leaves, and eat dandelions and other wild plants. Even a wounded soldier with one arm and one leg has to fight with a gun and hand-grenades. It was only the high morale among men and the perfect unity of the whole army that made us cling so stubbornly to the defense of the town."
Private First Class Hideo Fujino, Myitkyina, June 1945

USAAF bombs Japan

"The real terror for the people came with those leaflets naming the places to be bombed. When you did that and then bombed the places named, then there was real terror."

Dr. Kawai, chief editorial writer of the Nippon Times

With a range of 1,500 miles, the B-29 Superfortress had been designed specifically for the bombing of Japan. The first raid came from China on June 15, 1944. Then with the fall of Saipan, the first flight of 100 B-29s took off from the base there on November 12, 1944. It bombed Tokyo, the first air raid on the city since 1942.

At first, the bombing raids were ineffective. High-altitude strikes in daylight using high explosives did little damage to Japanese industry. Then the Commander of 20th Bomber Command, General Curtis E. LeMay, changed tactics. Low-level strikes at night using newly developed napalm proved successful. Tokyo is in an earthquake zone, and many of its building were made of wood and paper that caught fire easily. The first low-level attack on the night of March 9, 1945, destroyed around 25 percent of Tokyo, killing more than 80,000 people and leaving one million homeless. It is said that

Emperor Hirohito's viewing of the destroyed areas marked the beginning of his involvement in the peace process which culminated in Japan's surrender five months later. It was the first indication that Japan could be defeated without a costly invasion of the home islands.

OTHER ATTACKS

Similar attacks followed on 67 cities including Yokohama, Kobe, Osaka, Toyama, and Nagoya. As more islands fell into American hands, the bombing campaign was ramped up. By the end of the war, Japan was surrounded by the US and British navies, bombarding the ports. According to the Japanese government's official statistics, air attacks killed 260,000 people and destroyed 2,210,000 houses, leaving 9,200,000 homeless. However, like the Blitz and the destruction of German cities, the bombing campaign failed to crush the morale of the people.

American air raids (LEFT)
Aircraft carriers drop bombs on Hokadate, Japan.

Allied strikes on Japan (RIGHT)
Damage caused by incendiary night-time bombing, Honshu, Japan, 1944.

FEW AIR-RAID SHELTERS IN JAPAN

"The reason we had no definite policy of air-raid shelter protection for the citizens is that we did not unduly wish to alarm our citizens concerning the necessity for underground shelters as we feared it would interfere with normal routine life and have some effect on war production. We did encourage citizens who could afford it to build their own family air-raid shelters."

Abe Genki, Minister for Home Affairs, April to August, 1945

Red Army liberates
Auschwitz

Allied leaders meet at Yalta

Dresden destroyed
by firestorm

Allies cross the Rhine

Americans capture
Iwo Jima

Buchenwald liberated

Red Army reaches Berlin

Bergen-Belsen liberated

Hitler commits suicide

German unconditional
surrender in Italy;
Berlin surrenders

War in Europe ends

JANUARY   FEBRUARY   MARCH   APRIL   MAY   JUNE

1945

ALLIED VICTORY

WITH THE DEFEAT OF THE GERMAN WINTER OFFENSIVE IN THE WEST—KNOWN TO THE ALLIES AS "THE BATTLE OF THE BULGE"—GERMANY'S FATE WAS SEALED. JAPAN WAS NOW WITHIN RANGE OF US BOMBERS AND HAD NO EFFECTIVE AIR DEFENSES. AND STILL THE WAR DRAGGED ON, COSTING HUNDREDS OF THOUSANDS OF LIVES AND UNTOLD MISERY ON BOTH SIDES—BUT AN END WOULD COME, HOWEVER COSTLY.

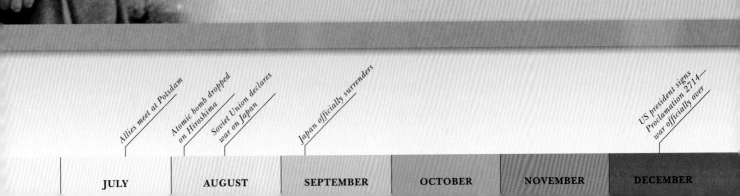

Allies meet at Potsdam

Atomic bomb dropped on Hiroshima

Soviet Union declares war on Japan

Japan officially surrenders

US president signs Proclamation 2714— war officially over

| JULY | AUGUST | SEPTEMBER | OCTOBER | NOVEMBER | DECEMBER |

Hitler—once an inspirational figure to the German people—was now feeble and deluded. With the enemy now on his doorstep, he put in place his plans to destroy what was left of Germany, rather than let the Allies on both fronts take it. He thought that the German people had betrayed him—they had failed to live up to the great destiny he had outlined for them. Those, such as Munitions Minister Albert Speer, who told him "the war is lost," were excluded from his inner circle. Convinced that he could stop the Russians at the gates of Berlin, Hitler took more and more power into his own hands and refused to listen to advice. "There is no need for you to try to teach me,"

he told Panzer pioneer General Heinz Guderian. "I've been commanding the Wehrmacht in the field for five years now and in that time I have had more practical experience than any of the gentlemen of the General Staff could ever hope for. I've studied Clausewitz and Moltke and read all the Schieffen papers. I'm more in the picture than you are." But there were still those fanatical soldiers who would fight to the end. In January 1945 an Order of the Day of the Sixth Panzer Army read as follows: "The true German soldier was and is the best in the world. Unwavering behind him is the Fatherland. And at the end is our Victory. Long live Germany: Heil to the Führer!"

Rocket attack (BELOW)
US Marines attack Japanese positions,
Iwo Jima, 1945.

SINGLE-HANDED AGAINST THE WORLD

The people of Japan were suffering under American bombing. The remaining Japanese troops abandoned on outlying islands were starving, but still—unable to comprehend defeat—they vowed to fight on. For many, death was preferable to the dishonor of surrender. After the Allied landings on Okinawa, Baron Kantaro Suzuki, a retired admiral and President of the Privy Council, was appointed Japanese Prime Minister. He had the unenviable task of trying to initiate peace talks at the behest of the Emperor, while risking assassination at the hands of the military establishment had they found out about it. Even after the deaths of Hitler and Mussolini, the Imperial General Staff announced its new policy of "Nippon single-handed against the world."

PLANS FOR THE POSTWAR WORLD

During the war, Churchill had traveled extensively to visit President Roosevelt and Marshal Stalin. In November 1943, the three leaders had met in Tehran, in Persia (Iran), to coordinate their invasion plans. In 1945, they would met again at Yalta in the Crimea to plan the shape of the postwar world.

Naval support (ABOVE)
Gunners aboard the USS Hornet *provide covering fire for an air raid on Tokyo, 1945.*

JAPAN'S PRIME MINISTER NEGOTIATES

"I was naturally in a very difficult position because, on one hand I had to carry out, to the best of my ability, the mission given to me by the Emperor to arrange for the conclusion of the war, whereas if anyone heard of this I would naturally have been attacked and probably killed by people who were opposed to such a policy. So that on one hand, I had to advocate an increase in war effort and determination to fight on, whereas through diplomatic channels and any means available, I had to try to negotiate with other countries to stop the war."

Baron Kantaro Suzuki, Japanese Prime Minister, April 7, 1945 to August 17, 1945

Auschwitz liberated

"We were no longer afraid of death; at any rate, not that death. Every bomb filled us with joy and gave us new confidence in life."

Elie Wiesel, Auschwitz survivor

The world already had some inkling of what had been happening to the Jews in the territories occupied by the Nazis. Jewish organizations had spoken out about the mass exterminations. Few believed that such an evil thing could be true, but when the Red Army liberated Auschwitz on January 27, 1945, the world was confronted by the terrible truth.

The largest of the Nazi camps, Auschwitz was near the town of Oswiecim in southern Poland. It consisted of three camps in one—a prison camp, a slave-labor camp, and an extermination camp designed to play a central role in the "final solution" because of the nearby railway junction that had 44 parallel tracks. Opened by the SS on April 27, 1940, Auschwitz I held political prisoners, mainly Germans and Poles. Work began on Auschwitz II, or Birkenau, in October 1941. This was the

extermination camp. It had 300 barracks, four "bathhouses" where prisoners were gassed, "corpse cellars" for storage, and "cremating ovens" for burning the bodies. Auschwitz III, opened in May 1942, supplied slave labor for the nearby chemical and synthetic-rubber plant of IG Farben.

GAS CHAMBERS

Arriving at Auschwitz, children and their mothers, along with the old and infirm, were taken directly to the gas chambers. Those exhausted by slave labor and the appalling conditions joined them, while camp doctors, including the notorious Josef Mengele, selected thousands of prisoners for cruel, crippling, and life-threatening experimentation. By 1944, so many were being killed that the bodies had to be burnt on huge pyres, fueled, partly, by the victims' own fat. When news of what was happening at Auschwitz leaked out, requests were made to the Allies to bomb the camp. Only the nearby factories were hit. As the Red Army advanced, the Germans evacuated Auschwitz and destroyed some of it. The inmates were taken on death marches to German camps to the west. More than one in four died from starvation or exposure, or were shot at the roadside. Between 1.1 and 1.5 million people died at Auschwitz. Ninety percent were Jews. Nineteen thousand were Gypsies. The Soviets found only 7,650 sick or starving prisoners still alive when they arrived at Auschwitz.

"Work makes one free" (LEFT)
The sign above the entrance to Auschwitz Concentration Camp, Poland.

Lives lost (RIGHT)
Discarded suitcases of Auschwitz victims.

The Allies meet at Yalta

"The peace of the world depends upon the lasting friendship of the three great powers."

Winston Churchill

Between February 4 and February 11, 1945, Roosevelt, Churchill, and Stalin met at Yalta in the Crimea to plan the final defeat of Germany and Japan. They discussed reparations, the occupation of the defeated nations, and the foundation of the United Nations. Although Roosevelt and Churchill thought that Stalin was negotiating in good faith, he would break most of the promises he made at Yalta.

The wartime Allies agreed to divide Germany into occupation zones, administered by the Soviet Union, the US, Britain, and France—though the French were denied a seat at the conference. War criminals were to be tried before an international criminal court. Stalin wanted $10 billion in reparations. The US and Britain were against this because they felt they would have to support Germany while the reparations were paid. Voting arrangements for the UN Security Council were agreed. Stalin agreed to join the war against Japan "two or three months" after the surrender of Germany—a secret protocol permitted the Soviets to reoccupy the territory lost to Japan in the Russo–Japanese War of 1904–05. In Eastern Europe, Stalin agreed to "interim governmental authorities broadly representative of all democratic elements in the population … and the earliest possible establishment through free elections of governments responsive to the will of the people."

POLAND

While Roosevelt and Churchill supported the Polish government in exile in London, the Soviets had set up a rival government in Lublin, eastern Poland. The Western Allies could only agree to recognize the Lublin government on the condition that it include representatives of other Polish political parties and hold free elections. These were never held, and Communist governments were installed in the countries of Poland, Hungary, Czechoslovakia, Romania, and Bulgaria. But

there was nothing the Western Allies could do to make Stalin live up to the promises he had made in Yalta. At the time, it was thought that the Red Army would be needed to defeat Japan, and the Soviet military occupied Eastern Europe.

Three great powers (RIGHT)
Winston Churchill, left, Franklin D. Roosevelt, center, and Joseph Stalin, right, at Yalta, the Crimea, 1945.

The fate of Europe (BELOW)
Diplomats from the Soviet Union, Britain and the USA discuss the future of post-war Europe, Yalta.

ROUND THE CONFERENCE TABLE

"Roosevelt was, above all else, a consummate politician. Few men could see more clearly their immediate objective, or show greater artistry in obtaining it ... Despite his knowledge of world affairs, he was always anxious to make it plain to Stalin that the United States was not 'ganging up' with Britain against Russia. The outcome of this was some confusion in Anglo-American relations which profited the Soviets ... Winston Churchill's strength lay in his vigorous sense of purpose and his courage. He was also generous and impulsive, but this could be a handicap at the conference table ... Marshal Stalin as a negotiator was the toughest proposition of all. If I had to pick a team for going into a conference room, Stalin would be my first choice."

Anthony Eden, British Foreign Secretary at Yalta

Dresden destroyed

"Dresden was at the time considered a military necessity by much more important people than myself, and … if their judgment was right the same arguments must apply to the ethics of bombing as a whole."

Air Marshal Arthur "Bomber" Harris

Before World War II, Dresden was one of Europe's most beautiful cities and known as "the Florence on the Elbe." On the night of February 13, 1945—just 12 weeks before the end of the war in Europe—it was bombed for the first time, causing a firestorm and massive loss of life. The question remains: was the raid really necessary?

Between February 13 and February 15, 1945, 1,300 heavy bombers dropped over 3,900 tons of high-explosive bombs and incendiary devices in four raids. The RAF bombed at night; the USAAF during the day. The resulting firestorm destroyed 13 square miles of the city center. Although the bombing had not been as intense as on other German cities, the old buildings were timber-framed and the cellars were connected, feeding air to the fire. The city was also completely unprepared for an attack and had few anti-aircraft defenses. It was estimated that between 35,000 and 135,000 people were killed. Nazi Propaganda Minister Joseph Goebbels inflated the number killed by a factor of ten, and issued a press release saying that Dresden had no war industries and was a city of culture. Goebbels and other leading Nazis wanted to use the bombing as an excuse to abandon the Geneva Convention on the Western Front. Raids on Dresden continued until April 17, though subsequent bombing did little more than churn the rubble.

JUSTIFICATION

The Allies justified the bombing of the city as a military and industrial target, a major rail transportation and communication center with 110 factories and 50,000 workers who were supporting the German war effort. Others have argued that Dresden was a cultural center of little or no military significance. Since the reunification of Germany in 1990, strenuous efforts have been made to rebuild the city to resemble how it once looked.

WHY DRESDEN WAS BOMBED

"In February of 1945, with the Russian Army threatening the heart of Saxony, I was called upon to attack Dresden; this was considered a target of the first importance for the offensive on the Eastern Front. Dresden had by this time become the main center of communications for the defense of Germany on the southern half of the Eastern Front and it was considered that a heavy air attack would disorganize these communications and also make Dresden useless as a controlling center for the defense. It was also by far the largest city in Germany, which had been left intact; it had never before been bombed. As a large center of war industry it was also of the highest importance."

Air Marshal Arthur "Bomber" Harris

Repairing the damage
Women help clear the rubble of Dresden to begin rebuilding, Germany, 1945.

Cautious advance (INSET)
Marines under fire gradually edge their way up the slopes of Mt. Suribachi, Iwo Jima, 1945.

Taking the hill (LEFT)
US troops triumphantly raise the American flag at the top of Mt. Suribachi.

Iwo Jima

"It was ghastly ... very little concealment. Few trees. No grass."

Marine Ted Allenby

The round trip of 3,000 miles from Saipan to mainland Japan was a long flight even for the US Superfortresses. But if US forces took the little volcanic island of Iwo Jima in the Bonin Islands, which lay some 760 miles southeast of Japan, they would halve the distance to Tokyo. With its fighters stationed there, the USAAF would be able to defend its bombers over their targets.

Iwo Jima was a doubly important target because Japan considered the island its "unsinkable aircraft carrier." It was a radar and fighter base whose aircraft intercepted the Superfortresses on their bombing missions over Japan. Irregularly shaped, Iwo Jima is about 5 miles long and anything from 800 yards to 2.5 miles wide. The Japanese were determined to hold on to it. They garrisoned the island with 21,000 troops under Lieutenant-General Kuribayashi Tadamichi, and it had the strongest defenses of all the Japanese possessions in the Pacific, making the best possible use of natural caves and the rocky terrain. For days before the landings, Iwo Jima was subjected to a massive US bombardment by naval guns, rockets, and air strikes using napalm. But the Japanese were so well dug in that no amount of shelling or bombing could knock them out.

RAISING THE FLAG

On February 19, 1945, 30,000 US Marines went ashore on the south of the island, sustaining 2,400 casualties. Their progress inland was slowed by the island's ashy volcanic soil. Having established a beachhead, the Marines then divided their forces. Half struck inland and took the first of the two Japanese airfields—a third was under construction. The other half turned south to take Mount Suribachi, an extinct volcano soon nicknamed Meatgrinder Hill for the casualties taken there. The Marines eventually took Mount Suribachi on February 23. The raising of the American flag on its summit was photographed by Joe Rosenthal of Associated Press. It became one of the best-

known images of the Pacific war. Divisions of Marines moved up the west and east coasts, but the fighting was so fierce that a third division, the floating reserve, had to be landed. It moved up the center of the island and by March 9 reached the northeast coast. On March 26 the Japanese staged their last suicidal attack with 350 men near Kitano Point on the northern tip of the island. After that, resistance collapsed. Some 20,000 Japanese were killed, the remaining 1,000 captured. US losses were 6,812 killed and 19,189 wounded. The Battle of Iwo Jima was a costly but decisive Allied victory. Now the all-out assault on the Japanese mainland could begin and, in the next five months, over 2,000 Superfortresses flew bombing missions over Japan from the airfields of Iwo Jima.

JAPANESE DELAY US FORCES

"Seeing that it was impossible to conduct our air, sea, and ground operations on Iwo Jima toward ultimate victory, it was decided that in order to gain time necessary for the preparation of the Homeland defense, our forces should rely solely upon the established defensive equipment in that area, checking the enemy by delaying tactics. ... It was a most depressing thought that we had no available means left for the exploitation of the strategic opportunities which might from time to time occur in the course of these operations."

Japanese staff officer

The Death of Mussolini

"Italy has need of a blood bath."

Benito Mussolini, 1913

Mussolini was by now merely a puppet in his Repubblica Sociale Italiana in northern Italy. However, Hitler was determined to defend his southern border—the Gothic Line established by Kesselring. At the height of the fighting in Normandy, Hitler dispatched there a battalion of Tiger tanks from France, seven divisions withdrawn from the Russian front and northern Europe, along with three new infantry divisions from Germany.

While the Germans were reinforcing in the south, the Allied strength in Italy was declining. Seven divisions were sent to Operation Dragoon. But between July 12 and July 15, Allied bombers destroyed all 23 road and rail bridges that cross the River Po. Air attacks also cut rail lines across northern Italy and on the Brenner Pass, effectively isolating Italy from the rest of Europe. With just 170 planes, mostly obsolete, the Luftwaffe could not attack Allies supply lines. Nevertheless, Kesselring had 26 divisions, including six Panzer divisions, while Alexander had just 20 divisions. However, wary of amphibious landings, Kesselring had to hold back six divisions to defend the Ligurian coast and the Gulf of Venice. Another two German-trained Italian divisions had to be held back to

fight what was turning into a civil war in Mussolini's republic, where partisans were attacking military depots and disrupting lines of communication. Even so, Kesselring was confident that he could hold the Gothic Line.

NEGOTIATED SURRENDER

The British launched an attack up the Italian east coast, while the Americans attacked in the mountains to the west. But after fierce fighting, the advance bogged down in the autumn rains. With not enough men, Kesselring proposed shortening the Gothic Line by withdrawing to the Alps. Hitler refused his permission and replaced Kesselring with Colonel-General Heinrich von Vietinghoff-Scheel. In the spring, the Allies resumed their massive airstrikes. In April, the British broke through. Ignoring Hitler's orders, Vietinghoff managed to evacuate most of his men across the Po. But his units were so fragmented and the command structure so disorganized that he asked for an armistice, which was granted on April 29. An unconditional surrender followed on May 2, the only negotiated surrender of the war. The war in Italy at least was over. Meanwhile Mussolini, trying to escape over the border into Switzerland disguised as a German soldier, had been captured by partisans. On April 28, 1945, he and his mistress Claretta Petacci were shot and killed. Their bodies were hung upside down from lampposts in the Piazza Loreto in Milan. Few Italians mourned his passing. He had dragged his country into a disastrous war that it was ill-prepared and unwilling to fight. Democracy returned after 20 years of dictatorship and, when a neo-fascist party espousing Mussolini's ideology stood in the 1948 elections, it won just 2 percent of the vote.

RAIN STOPS ATTACK

"Rain, which was at the time spoiling the Fifth Army's attack on Bologna, now reached a high pitch of intensity. On October 26 all the bridges over the Savio, in our immediate rear, were swept away and our small bridgeheads over the Ronco were eliminated and destroyed."

Field Marshal Harold Alexander

Mussolini rescued by Germans
The former dictator, with high-ranking German officers, inspects a newly formed Italian (Fascist) division, some months after being "rescued" from the hotel where he was held prisoner.

Roosevelt dies

"He slipped away this afternoon. He did his job to the end as he would have wanted."

Eleanor Roosevelt in a message to their four sons serving in the armed forces

US President Franklin Delano Roosevelt had been one of the great architects of the Allied fightback during the war. When he came to power in 1933, the United States had been determinedly isolationist. But he had seen the dangers of the rise of Fascism and Nazism in Europe and militarism in Japan, and he contributed significant American force to rid the world of the enemies of democracy.

Elected to the New York State senate as a Democrat at the age of 28, Roosevelt moved into Federal politics, serving as Assistant Secretary for the Navy during World War I. An advocate of the League of Nations, he was the Democratic vice-presidential nominee in the 1920 presidential election. The following year he was struck down with poliomyelitis and never regained the use of his legs. But in 1928 he was elected governor of New York. In 1932—during the Great Depression—he won the presidential election, offering a "new deal" for the American people. Although many considered him dangerously left-wing, his policies ameliorated the worst of the hardship brought on by the Great Depression. He won re-election in 1936 with an increased majority.

WARTIME LEADER

In 1940, Roosevelt broke with the traditional two-term presidency observed since George Washington and won a third term on the promise that he would keep America out of the war, though he also pledged to make the US the "Arsenal of Democracy." He formed a close relationship with Churchill and did everything short of declaring war to support Britain. He signed the Atlantic Charter, which outlined Britain and America's war aims, before the US had joined the hostilities. When the Japanese attack on Pearl Harbor on December 7,

1941, eventually forced America into the fray, he was a resolute leader. As commander-in-chief, he won an unprecedented fourth term in the US presidency. At 3.35 pm on April 12, 1945, Roosevelt died of a cerebral hemorrhage at his holiday cottage in Warm Springs, Georgia. Although Roosevelt died when Allied victory was just weeks away, at Yalta he had helped draw the blueprint for the postwar world and the establishment of the United Nations. Roosevelt was succeeded by his vice-president, Harry S. Truman.

HARRY S. TRUMAN

A veteran of World War I, Truman worked his way up the Democratic political ladder in Missouri, becoming the state's junior senator in 1935. Winning a second term in 1940, he gained national prominence by exposing waste and fraud in the US military. In the 1944 US presidential election, Roosevelt picked him as a running mate. During Truman's 82 days as vice-president, Truman met the president only twice and Roosevelt, who did not acknowledge how ill he was, did little to inform him of the situation or his plans. Sworn in as president at 19:09 hours on April 12, Truman was about to face one of the most crucial decisions of the war.

Roosevelt funeral (LEFT)
The body of US President Franklin D. Roosevelt, with honor guard, passes the White House, Washington, DC, USA, 1945.

Truman as US President (INSET)
US President Truman announces Japan's surrender, 1945.

TRUMAN'S REACTION

"I don't know whether you fellows ever had a load of hay fall on you, but when they told me yesterday what had happened, I felt like the moon, the stars, and all the planets had fallen on me."

President Harry S. Truman, addressing journalists, April 13, 1945

Liberating the camps

"The most horrible, frightful place I have ever seen. I am told thirty thousand prisoners died in the last few months. I can well believe the figure."

British senior medical officer, Belsen

The Allies had known about the concentration camps, but nothing could have prepared the Allied troops when they liberated the camps of Buchenwald, near Weimar, and Bergen-Belsen, near Celle, in April 1933. Starved corpses had been left to rot in heaps. Disease was rampant and the conditions were so bad for those still alive that thousands died even after the Allies rushed food and medical assistance to them.

The first and biggest of the concentration camps, Buchenwald had housed 240,000 prisoners from at least 30 countries. More than 43,000 died at Buchenwald, while over 10,000 were shipped from there to extermination camps. On April 6, 1945, the Germans evacuated around 28,500 prisoners for the death march on which one in four died. When US troops arrived on April 11, the guards had fled. The troops found 20,000 prisoners remaining, some 2,500 in such a pitiful condition that they could not survive. There were some 900 boys under 14, whose parents were dead or among the millions of refugees wandering through the ruins of Europe. American doctors fed the boys on milk because they were unable to digest solid food. The troops found a lampshade made for the commandant's wife from tattooed human skin, shrunken heads, brass-studded lashes, and a portable gallows. Some prisoners complained of having been the victims of medical experiments in which Nazi doctors operated on them without anesthetics.

ANNE FRANK

On April 15, 1945, near where they had crossed the Rhine, British troops found a concentration camp between the villages of Bergen and Belsen. It had been designed for 10,000 but it then held 41,000. Like Buchenwald, this was not an extermination camp—there were no gas chambers there—but some 37,000 prisoners had died from starvation, overwork, and disease, and their corpses had been bulldozed into mass graves. Anne Frank, whose wartime diary would later become world-famous, died of typhus at Bergen-Belsen in March 1945, while the Allied armies were a matter of miles away. Many of the survivors were beyond help, suffering from starvation, typhus, typhoid, and tuberculosis. Some were so emaciated they were barely recognizable as human. Huge heaps of corpses had been left to rot. In one compound, there was a heap of naked women's bodies measuring 90 feet by 240 feet, and 4 feet high. Children played nearby. Despite the best efforts of Allied troops, 600 fresh victims had to be buried every day until the evacuation of the camp could be arranged.

Buchenwald (LEFT)
Forced laborers at the Buchenwald Concentration Camp near Jena, Germany.

Bergen-Belsen (RIGHT)
*One of several mass graves found at the
concentration camp, 1945.*

Delousing procedure (BELOW)
*Liberated women prisoners from Bergen-Belsen are
dusted with DDT by a British trooper, 1945.*

Berlin falls

"It will take the Russians exactly two hours and fifteen minutes to capture Berlin—two hours laughing their heads off and fifteen minutes to break down the barricades."

A joke passed around among the two million inhabitants of "Fortress Berlin"

Churchill wanted the British to take Berlin as the "supreme symbol of defeat," but it was not his call. Eisenhower decided that the Allies should make a thrust through southern Germany to prevent the remains of the German Army falling back to the "National Redoubt" in Bavaria, where the Nazis hoped to regroup and continue the war.

Having fought their way over 1,400 miles from Stalingrad in just over two years, the Red Army under General Zhukov drew up in front of Berlin. At 04:00 hours on April 14, 1945, they began the biggest artillery barrage ever mounted on the Eastern Front. Mortars, tanks, self-propelled guns, light and heavy artillery—along with 400 Katyusha multiple rocket

Allied troops in Berlin (ABOVE)
A bronze bust of Hitler, outside the Reichstag, 1945.

Hitler's HQ in ruins (LEFT)
The Chancellory Gardens, where Hitler's remains were burned, 1945.

launchers—all pounded the German positions. Men were deafened by the guns and shook uncontrollably. Then, after 35 minutes of artillery pounding, the Soviets attacked. In his fortified bunker under the *Reichschancellory*, Hitler still believed that he could win. He predicted the Russians would suffer their greatest defeat at the gates of Berlin. His maps told him so. They were still covered in little flags representing SS and Germany Army units. Unfortunately, the units they represented had long since ceased to exist or were so chronically understrength that they were next to useless. Anyone who pointed this out to Hitler was dismissed. What Propaganda Minister Joseph Goebbels now called "Fortress Berlin" was defended by 90,000 ill-equipped boys from the Hitler Youth and elderly men from the *Volkssturm*, or Home Guard.

LINK-UP ON THE ELBE
In charge of the German defense was Colonel-General Gotthard Heinrici, who had pulled his frontline troops back so that Zhukov's massive bombardment fell on empty positions.

Hitler's bunker (LEFT)
Allied soldiers inspect the ruins of the Reichschancellory, Berlin, 1945.

When they advanced, Zhukov's men suffered terrible casualties. Stalin, who had assured Eisenhower that Berlin had "lost its former strategic importance," diverted a second army under General Ivan Koniev to march on Berlin in a pincer movement. To ensure that the Americans would not come and snatch their prize at the last moment, both Zhukov and Koniev sent forces to meet US units at Torgau on the River Elbe on April 25. Himmler, Goebbels, and other leading Nazis left the city. Hitler refused to go, pretending, for a while, that the situation could be reversed. He issued a barrage of orders to his nonexistent armies while 15,000 Russians guns pounded the city. As Soviet troops entered Berlin, Hitler sacked his designated successor Göring for trying to take over the Nazi leadership, and Himmler, for trying to put out peace feelers to the British and Americans. Grand Admiral Karl Dönitz was named as Hitler's new successor. Then Hitler received news that Mussolini was dead. On April 29, Hitler married his mistress Eva Braun. The following day, he dictated his will and his final political testament. That afternoon, in their private quarters, Hitler and his wife of one day committed suicide. Their bodies were burned in a shallow trench in the Chancellory Gardens.

Germany surrenders

"With this signature, the German people and the German Armed Forces are, for better or worse, delivered into the victors' hands."

General Alfred Jodl, Army Chief of Staff, Rheims, May 7, 1945

By the time Hitler died, Red Army troops under both Zhukov and Koniev were in Berlin. But Koniev was ordered to halt so that Zhukov's men would have the honor of raising the Red Flag over the Reichstag. Zhukov's subsequent popularity was seen as a threat by Stalin, who banished him to obscurity in 1946.

The Soviets accepted the unconditional surrender of General Weidling in Berlin on May 2. The surrender of the German forces in northwestern Europe was signed at General Montgomery's tent on Lüneburg Heath on May 4. Another surrender document, covering all the German forces, was signed with more ceremony at Eisenhower's headquarters in Rheims at 02:41 hours on May 7 and ratified in Berlin the following day. At midnight on May 8, 1945, the war in Europe was officially over.

THE FATE OF BERLIN

It is not known how many people perished in the Battle of Berlin. Estimates put the number of German dead as high as 200,000 and the Russian dead at 150,000. The Soviet troops then went on an orgy of drinking, looting, and raping. It is thought that as many as 100,000 women were raped—often publicly—in the aftermath of the war in Berlin, and an estimated two million in the whole of eastern Germany. Stalin believed his men should have their reward. Russian soldiers often shot their victims afterwards. Other women committed suicide. In one district of Berlin alone, 215 female suicides were recorded in three weeks. At the Yalta conference in the Crimea in February 1945 the agreement was that Berlin would be divided between the four powers—Britain, France, the US, and the Soviet Union. By the time the Four Power Control Commission arrived to take control, the Russian orgy was over. Almost immediately, the Cold War started. The part of the city in the hands of the western powers became West Berlin, which over the years became an enclave of democracy and free-market capitalism deep inside the region dominated by the Soviet Union. The Soviet dominance extended, by common consent, 100 miles to the west of the capital. This was a bone of contention for the next 55 years, until the reunification of Germany in 1990.

Peace in Europe (LEFT)
General Willhelm Keitel signs Germany's surrender at Soviet HQ, Berlin, Germany, 1945.

Germany falls (RIGHT)
An exhausted German soldier waves the white flag and surrenders at gunpoint, 1945.

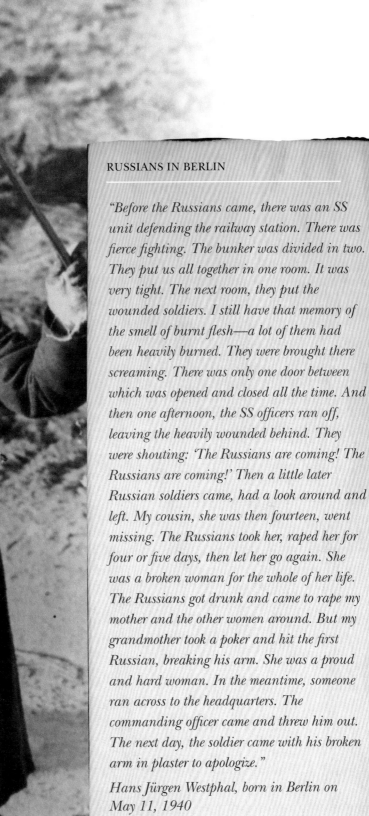

RUSSIANS IN BERLIN

"Before the Russians came, there was an SS unit defending the railway station. There was fierce fighting. The bunker was divided in two. They put us all together in one room. It was very tight. The next room, they put the wounded soldiers. I still have that memory of the smell of burnt flesh—a lot of them had been heavily burned. They were brought there screaming. There was only one door between which was opened and closed all the time. And then one afternoon, the SS officers ran off, leaving the heavily wounded behind. They were shouting: 'The Russians are coming! The Russians are coming!' Then a little later Russian soldiers came, had a look around and left. My cousin, she was then fourteen, went missing. The Russians took her, raped her for four or five days, then let her go again. She was a broken woman for the whole of her life. The Russians got drunk and came to rape my mother and the other women around. But my grandmother took a poker and hit the first Russian, breaking his arm. She was a proud and hard woman. In the meantime, someone ran across to the headquarters. The commanding officer came and threw him out. The next day, the soldier came with his broken arm in plaster to apologize."

Hans Jürgen Westphal, born in Berlin on May 11, 1940

VE Day celebrations

"We may allow ourselves a brief period of rejoicing; but let us not forget for a moment the toil and efforts that lie ahead. Japan, with all her treachery and greed, remains unsubdued. We must now devote all our strength and resources to the completion of our task, both at home and abroad."

Winston Churchill, BBC broadcast, May 8, 1945

Suddenly the war in Europe was over. Massive celebrations took place in Chicago, Los Angeles, and especially in New York City's Times Square. However, flags in the US remained at half mast in mourning for President Roosevelt, to whom President Truman dedicated the victory. But in Britain, after nearly six years of hardship and suffering, wartime drabness and privation were forgotten, temporarily at least, and celebrations knew no bounds.

By midday on May 8, 1945, Whitehall and the Mall were packed with people, many dressed in red, white, and blue, who cheered as Churchill drove by to lunch at Buckingham Palace, though no official announcement had yet been made. At 15:00 hours, the crowd fell silent as Churchill's broadcast from the cabinet war rooms was played over loudspeakers in Trafalgar Square and Parliament Square. He confirmed that the ceasefire had been signed at 02:41 hours in Rheims the previous day. In his broadcast he paid tribute to the men and women who had laid down their lives for victory as well as to all those who had "fought valiantly" on land, sea, and in the air.

"FOR HE'S A JOLLY GOOD FELLOW"

Fifty thousand people in Whitehall and on the Mall celebrated by hugging one another, kissing strangers, blowing whistles, dancing, and throwing confetti. A long "hokey-cokey" line snaked around Queen Victoria's statue at the end of the Mall before Buckingham Palace. There was a huge cheer as the king, queen, and the two princesses appeared on the balcony. In Whitehall, crowds cheered themselves hoarse when Winston Churchill appeared on the balcony of the Ministry of Health, cigar in mouth, waving his famous "V for victory" salute. The

Guards' band struck up "For He's A Jolly Good Fellow," then Churchill sang and conducted the crowd in "Land Of Hope And Glory." Even after dark, thousands of people continued to converge on some of London's great monuments, floodlit specially for the occasion. There were fireworks, too, and effigies of Hitler were burned on bonfires around the capital.

CELEBRATING IN TRAFALGAR SQUARE

"When the announcement came a friend and I decided to go to London … We waited until it was nearly dark and went on a tram to London Bridge. There were bonfires on some of the bomb sites and lights in some of the shops. Arriving once again to a very crowded Trafalgar Square we could see Nelson lit up by a searchlight. We pushed our way into the square but a car was in our way. As I went around it a girl in uniform tripped and literally fell at my feet. I picked her up and with a big smile she planted a kiss full on my mouth … I will always remember my first real kiss!"

Ken Hulme, then 14

Allies victorious (LEFT)
*Winston Churchill and members of
the Royal Family wave from the
balcony of Buckingham Palace.*

Joy in New York City (BELOW)
*Thousands of people gather to
celebrate VE Day in Times Square,
New York City, 1945.*

Peace at Potsdam

"It is the intention of the Allies that the German people be given
the opportunity to prepare for the eventual reconstruction of their
life on a democratic and peaceful basis."

Potsdam Declaration, August 2, 1945

Between July 17 and August 2, 1945, the Allies met once again, in the Cecilienhof Palace in the Berlin suburb of Potsdam, to discuss the future of Europe and the prosecution of the war against Japan. The Soviet Union was represented by Stalin, the US, for the first time by President Truman. During the conference, Churchill was voted out of office and was replaced by his former deputy Clement Attlee.

It had already been decided at Yalta that Germany was to be divided into four zones, occupied by the British, Americans, Soviets, and French. Now Berlin, Vienna, and Austria were also to be divided into four zones. Each Allied nation would take reparations from its own zone, while the Soviet Union was allowed 10 to 15 percent of the machinery of the western zone in exchange for agricultural products and raw materials from the east. An Allied Control Council made up of representatives of the four allies would be in overall charge. Its aims were summed up by the "five Ds"—denazification, demilitarization, democratization, decentralization, and deindustrialization. The Soviet Union would take some of the territory of Poland, while Poland's western border would now be extended to the line of the Oder and Neisse rivers, engulfing East Prussia. Millions of Germans would have to move. Communists already controlled the governments of Hungary, Bulgaria, and Romania—all "liberated" by the Red Army—and Stalin would brook no Western interference. Churchill was suspicious of Stalin's motives, but soon found that he was in no position to do anything about it.

A NEW WEAPON

The atomic bomb was tested successfully in New Mexico on July 16. During the Potsdam Conference, Truman told Stalin that the US had a "new weapon." However, no mention was made of it when the Allies issued an ultimatum on July 26, 1945, demanding Japan's unconditional surrender and threatening an escalation of the bombing campaign.

CHURCHILL'S FALL

The US presidential elections had continued during World War II. But in Britain there had been no election since 1935. Churchill had led a wartime coalition government with members from all parties. But with the war in Europe now over, the Labour Party split from the coalition and an election was called. Although Churchill remained personally popular, the British people wanted a change. The Labour Party won by a landslide and its leader Clement Attlee became prime minister. Churchill, though shaken, drove to Buckingham Palace on July 26, where he told the king: "The decision has been recorded. I have therefore laid down the charge which was placed upon me in darker times." Unlike other former prime ministers, he refused a peerage—though he was later knighted—and remained in the House of Commons as leader of the opposition. He toured the US, warning of the "iron curtain" that had descended across Europe. In the British general election of 1951, he was returned to power and remained prime minister until 1955. In 1963, he was made an honorary US citizen by act of Congress, the only person to be so honored. When he died in 1965, the British gave him a state funeral.

Rebuilding Europe (RIGHT)
Allies discuss the fate of Germany and Europe at Potsdam, Germany, 1945.

Map of Germany (INSET)
Partition of Germany, 1945.

83

❶ *British Zone*
❷ *French Zone*
❸ *American Zone*
❹ *Russian Zone*
❺ *Berlin divided into four zones*

PARTITION OF GERMANY, 1945

The battle for Borneo

"While we were dug in, in our positions in the mountains, several Australians came up to the mouth of our holes and tossed in a couple of hand grenades. One needs lots of courage to do that."

Lieutenant-Colonel Yasuse Shibazaki

While US forces consolidated their positions in the Philippines, the Australians began the reconquest of Borneo with the support of the US Seventh Fleet, the Australian First Tactical Air Force, and the US Thirteenth Air Force. It would be the last major combined operation of the war in the southwest Pacific and would prove to be controversial.

KINDNESS OF AUSTRALIAN TROOPS

"The only time I met any enemy soldier was after the end of the war, and they were Australians. I felt that the troops I was fighting against were sincere in everything they did. They were glad the fighting was over. They knew what our situation was. The Aussies showed much kindness towards us, much more than we ever expected. Our troops at the close of the war were weak and sick. The Australian government produced timber and other material for us to construct a field hospital. The Australian government was very kind to us; so was each individual soldier. Their government provided transportation to ship clothes from Rabaul … What we had on was in rags. A third of the men had no shoes."

Lieutenant-Colonel Yasuse Shibazaki, Japanese garrison, Balikpapan

The Borneo Campaign
Australian soldiers fire at Japanese positions during an attempt to retake the island of Borneo, 1945.

The campaign opened on April 12, 1944, with the Allied bombardment of the small island of Tarakan, off the northeast coast of Borneo. The aim of this operation was to secure the island's airstrip to provide air cover for landings at Brunei and Balikpapan. On April 30, the Australians landed on nearby Sadau Island in the Baragan Straits. From there they could shell Tarakan's beach fortifications. They landed on Tarakan itself on May 1. After four days of fighting the town of Tarakan fell to the Allies at a cost of 225 Australians killed and 669 wounded. Some 1,540 Japanese were dead. While it had been expected that it would take only a few weeks to secure Tarakan and reopen the airstrip, the fighting on the island lasted until June 19 and the airstrip was not opened until June 28. By then, the Australians had already successfully landed on Brunei, so the costly operation on Tarakan was generally considered worthwhile. While Brunei was taken quickly, the Japanese garrison on the island of Labuan held out for over a week. After the Australians had secured Brunei Bay, supported by further landings and indigenous Dayak fighters operating as guerrillas, they advanced rapidly against weak Japanese resistance, and most of northwest Borneo was liberated by the end of the war.

BALIKPAPAN

The next Allied objective was the town of Balikpapan on the central east coast of Borneo, because the town provided oil supplies for Japanese troops in the south of the island. This operation was opposed by the Australian commander General Sir Thomas Blamey, who thought it unnecessary but went

ahead on the orders of General MacArthur. After a 20-day Allied bombardment, Australian troops landed near the town on July 1. Balikpapan and its surroundings were secured after some heavy fighting on July 21, but mopping up continued until the end of the war. The fall of Balikpapan duly deprived the Japanese of their oil supplies. The British then began preparing an advance base there for the retaking of Singapore. But by the time the air base on Borneo was built, Japan had surrendered. Although the Borneo Campaign was criticized as pointless or a waste of the soldiers' lives, it succeeded in freeing Allied prisoners of war, who were being held in deteriorating conditions.

Okinawa

"After Coral Sea and Midway I still had hope; and after Guadalcanal I felt we could not win, only that we were not going to lose. After the Marianas, we had little chance. After Okinawa, it was all over."

Captain Ohmae, Chief of Staff, Japanese Southeastern Fleet (Rabaul)

Despite the success of the bombing campaign against Japan, the Allied invasion plans were not discarded immediately. There would be one more "island hop" before the end of the war. It would be the largest amphibious operation of the Pacific war. Its objective was Okinawa, an island some 70 miles long and 7 miles wide just 350 miles south of Kyushu—the last stepping-stone before the invasion of Japan itself.

American reconnaissance planes put the strength of Okinawa's garrison at 65,000. In fact, it was almost 120,000 strong. Some 10,000 aircraft defended the island, though hundreds were destroyed on the ground by an air raid on March 18, and the Japanese Imperial Navy, though short of fuel, sent a task force headed by the *Yamato*, the largest battleship ever built. Facing the Imperial Navy was the largest array of battle-hardened troops yet deployed in the Pacific: three Marine Divisions and four Army Divisions—over 155,000

men in all. But by the time the fighting was finished, over 300,000 Americans had been committed to the action. Over 1,300 vessels of all sizes, including a large British carrier fleet, were assembled for the landing. On April 1, the island was bombarded with 44,825 five-inch shells, 32,000 rockets, and 22,500 mortar rounds. The Allied troops clambered into their landing craft at 04:00 hours for the four-and-a-half-hour run into Hagushi beach on the west coast of the island, which had just been cleared of mines. They hit the beaches at 08:30 hours and found, to their surprise, no opposition. By nightfall, 60,000 men were ashore. The next day US troops drove across the island to the east coast. The north of the island was cleared of Japanese forces by April 21, killing 2,500 defenders at a cost of 218 Americans killed and 902 wounded.

MASSIVE CASUALTIES

On April 4, the Americans reached the southern defenses at Shuri, where the Japanese would make a fight of it. Even with reinforcements, US troops could not dent the defenses. Although the Japanese suffered ten times the American casualty rate, on April 12 they went on the offensive. For two days, they sent in wave after wave of suicidal attacks. All were repulsed. The Allied bombardment was stepped up on the fortified hills and ridges, which had been given names such as Chocolate

Hills of Okinawa (LEFT)
A US Army flame-throwing tank in action, Okinawa, Japan, 1945.

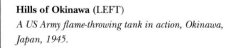

Launching the attack (RIGHT)
A US landing ship fires a barrage of rockets, just before the invasion of Okinawa Island, 1945.

Ground forces (LEFT)
US Marines attempt to locate and draw out a Japanese sniper, Wana Ridge, Japan, 1945.

Drop and Sugar Loaf by the US troops who risked, and often lost, their lives to take them. On May 2 the Japanese went on the offensive again but were driven back, losing 5,000 men. Fearing they were about to be encircled, they pulled back on May 21 to the southern tip of the island. A rainstorm covered the retreat and grounded the Allied planes on their aircraft carriers. By the time Shuri fell to the Allies on May 31, it had been reduced to rubble. The Marines made another amphibious landing, using flame-throwers and high explosives to clear enemy positions. On June 21, the Japanese commander knelt outside his

headquarters and committed suicide by *hara-kiri*. Scorning an American offer of surrender, his final order was that his men revert to guerrilla warfare. They continued fighting until the end of the month when some 7,400 gave themselves up, the first time the Japanese had surrendered in large numbers. At least 110,000 Japanese soldiers were dead, along with many civilians. For the Allies it was the costliest operation in the Pacific. US ground forces had lost 7,203 killed and 31,807 wounded. Attacked by *kamikaze* planes, the navy had lost some 5,000 killed and a similar number wounded. Twenty-seven Japanese suicide pilots penetrated the wall of fire put up by the escorts, damaging four aircraft carriers, knocking out the USS *Franklin* and the *Wasp*, and hitting a battleship, a cruiser, four destroyers, and six other ships. Japan had lost what remained of its navy, and 7,800 Japanese aircraft had been destroyed for the loss of 763 Allied planes. The Japanese home islands now lay wide open to advances by Allied forces.

Nuclear war

"If the radiance of a thousand suns were to
burst at once into the sky, that would be like
the splendor of the mighty one. Now I am
become Death, the destroyer of worlds."

J. Robert Oppenheimer quoting from the
Bhagavad Gita, *July 16, 1945*

On August 2, 1939, Albert Einstein, a German citizen who emigrated to America when Hitler came to power in 1933, wrote to President Roosevelt, warning him that the Germans might soon be capable of building a weapon of devastating power utilizing atomic fission. Although a lifelong pacifist, Einstein urged Roosevelt to begin research to ensure that the West had an atomic bomb first.

THE MANHATTAN PROJECT

The British had already learnt how to make an atomic bomb by enriching natural uranium. But it was a slow, difficult, and expensive process. In utmost secrecy, they asked Canada for uranium and America for its help. In June 1940, President Roosevelt set up the National Defense Research Committee whose subcommittee, known as the Uranium Section, looked into the possibilities of atomic power. Meanwhile, to keep them safe from the bombing, the British moved their scientists to Montreal, where they worked with Canadian and French colleagues. It soon became clear that only the US could afford to produce the quantity of Uranium-235 required. The US Congress voted two billion dollars over four years without knowing the exact nature of the project. In 1942, the Manhattan Project was set up under General Leslie Groves, and employed British and American

scientists under J. Robert Oppenheimer. It got its name from its first home, the Corps of Engineers' Manhattan Engineer District Office.

LOS ALAMOS

After the expatriate-Italian scientist Enrico Fermi initiated a nuclear chain reaction at the University of Chicago, the project was moved to a laboratory city built at Los Alamos, New Mexico, where further research could be undertaken in secrecy. Over 140,000 people worked on the project and, on July 16, 1945—two months after Germany had surrendered—the first atomic bomb was exploded at the nearby Alamogordo Bombing Range.

THE DROPPING OF THE ATOMIC BOMB

Within 24 hours of President Roosevelt's death, President Truman was told about the Manhattan Project by Secretary of War Henry Stimson. He was also reading military assessments that the invasion of Japan, now scheduled for 1946, would cost as many as one million casualties, given the use of kamikazes and the suicidal defense of Iwo Jima and Okinawa.

The atomic bomb that was tested successfully in a desert area at Alamogordo had an explosive power equivalent to that of more than 15,000 tons of TNT—vastly more devastating than any previous weapon. Truman realized that it might be used to bomb Japan into surrender rather than waste more American lives in the invasion of the Japanese homeland. The Allies had received no reply to the ultimatum they had sent to the Japanese from Potsdam. So on August 6, 1945, an atomic bomb was loaded onto a specially equipped B-29 Superfortress called *Enola Gay* on Tinian Island in the Marianas. It flew to Japan and, at 08:15 hours local time, dropped the bomb on Hiroshima, at the southern end of Honshu Island. The combined heat and blast obliterated everything in the immediate vicinity. Fires burned out over four square miles of the city. Between 70,000 and 80,000 people were dead or dying and over 70,000 others were injured—though as many, if not more, were killed by conventional bombing and shelling that same day. When this devastation did not prompt a surrender, a second bomb was dropped on Nagasaki on August 9. This killed between 35,000 and 40,000 people.

THE SOVIET UNION DECLARES WAR

The Japanese government found it difficult to comprehend the power of the new weapon. A key factor in their decision to surrender was the declaration of war by the Soviet Union on Japan on August 8, threatening Japan's huge army now cut off on the mainland of Asia. Even so, militarists in the Japanese government planned a coup to prevent capitulation.

Fires over the city (ABOVE)
Mushroom cloud over Nagasaki, Japan, 1945.

The second bomb (INSET)
Nagasaki devastated, Japan, 1945.

Japan surrenders

"As far as the army is concerned, the termination of the war was declared by the Emperor and not by the army."

Major-General Miwa

Japan had always envisaged a negotiated end to the Greater East Asia War—but had imagined that it would come when its "Greater East Asia Co-prosperity Sphere" was at its height, not when the cities of the homeland were a blackened ruin. However, there were many in the military who wanted to fight on—whatever the cost.

After the fall of Saipan on July 7, 1944, and the beginning of the US bombing, the Japanese were faced with the prospect of an invasion of the home islands. According to the War Journal of the Imperial Headquarters, there was only one honorable course of action. "We can no longer direct the war with any hope of success," it concluded. "The only course left is for Japan's 100 million people to sacrifice their lives by charging the enemy to make them lose the will to fight." On June 22, 1945, following the fall of Okinawa, the emperor told the six-man Supreme War Guidance Council that he

wanted to end the war. They made overtures to the Soviet Union with whom they still maintained a non-aggression pact. However, the "unconditional surrender" insisted upon by the US and Britain was unacceptable to the Japanese; consequently, they rejected the Potsdam ultimatum.

Both the Japanese Army and Navy had been working on atomic programs themselves. They knew how difficult it would be to build an atomic bomb and doubted that the Americans could do it. After the bomb was dropped on Hiroshima on August 6, Japanese military opinion was that the Americans were unlikely to have more than one bomb. More distressing had been the declaration of war by the Soviet Union on

Japan surrenders (BELOW)
The surrender ceremony aboard the USS Missouri, *September 2, 1945.*

August 8. Within two days, the Red Army had advanced 120 miles, taking one million prisoners. After the bomb was dropped on Nagasaki on August 9, the Supreme War Guidance Council was still split three against three on the matter of surrender. But the Emperor insisted on surrender.

JAPAN SURRENDERS

On August 10, the Japanese government agreed to surrender to the terms offered at Potsdam on the understanding that they could retain their emperor and the institution he represented. The Allies agreed. On the night of August 14, there was an attempted military coup, but the conspirators failed to find the surrender broadcast that the emperor had taped, and killed themselves. The following day, August 15, the Japanese people heard the voice of Emperor Hirohito on the radio for the first time. He urged the Japanese people to accept the unacceptable. The US occupation of Japan began on August 28 and, on September 2, General MacArthur formally accepted the Japanese surrender on the deck of Admiral Nimitz's flagship, the USS *Missouri*, in Tokyo Bay. World War II was over. However, this did not mean that the fighting had stopped. The Russians fought on into September to take the Kuril Islands. Japanese forces in southeast Asia surrendered in Singapore on September 12. In remote areas, some Japanese soldiers did not lay down their arms until early 1946; others refused to surrender at all because it was against the code of *bushido*.

Much of southeast Asia was still in Japanese hands when the surrender came and, in places, the Allies had to use the Japanese troops there to maintain order.

An end to the war (ABOVE)

Fighter planes fly in formation during surrender ceremonies, Tokyo, Japan.

PRISONERS OF WAR

The Japanese had taken over 140,000 Allied prisoners of war and civilians living in the Far East and uncountable numbers of Chinese and indigenous prisoners. When the camps were liberated, it was discovered that prisoners had been treated with appalling cruelty. One in three had died from starvation, overwork, punishment, execution, or disease. Prisoners were put to work in mines, fields, shipyards, and factories on a diet of about 600 calories a day. The worst treatment was handed out to the 61,000 men who built the Burma–Siam (Thailand) railroad.

War crimes trials

"The privilege of opening the first trial in history for crimes against the peace of the world imposes a grave responsibility. The wrongs we seek to condemn and punish have been so calculated, so malignant, and so devastating that civilization cannot tolerate their being ignored."

US chief prosecutor Justice Jackson

Churchill was not in favor of the war crimes trials. He thought the leading Nazis should simply be executed. However, at the conference held at Yalta in February 1945, Britain, America, and the Soviet Union had agreed to prosecute the Nazi leaders and other war criminals. Later, Japanese militarists and those accused of committing atrocities in the Far East also stood trial.

An International Military Tribunal was given the authority to indict offenders on three counts: crimes against peace, crimes against humanity, and violations of the laws of war. Each of the four Allied powers provided one judge and a prosecutor, and procedures followed Anglo-American practice. The tribunal first sat on October 18, 1945, in the Supreme Court in Berlin, where the prosecution entered indictments against 24 Nazi leaders and six "criminal organizations"—Hitler's cabinet, the leadership corps of the Nazi Party, the SS (party police) and SD (security police), the Gestapo, the SA (Nazi stormtroopers), and the General Staff and High Command of the Army. On November 20, 1945, the tribunal moved to the Nuremberg Palace of Justice, which had a large, undamaged prison attached. On October 1, 1946, the verdict was handed down on 22 of the original defendants. The organizer of slave labor, Robert Ley, had committed suicide in jail, and the armaments manufacturer Gustav Krupp was too ill to appear and charges against him were dropped. Sentenced to death and hanged in the early morning of October 16, 1946, were the following: the governor-general of Poland Hans Frank; minister of internal affairs Wilhelm Frick; Hitler's strategic adviser Alfred Jodl; head of the SD Ernst Kaltenbrunner; Field Marshal Wilhelm Keitel; Foreign Minister Joachim von Ribbentrop; Minister for the Occupied Territories Alfred Rosenberg; another organizer of forced labor Fritz Sauckel; anti-Semitic propagandist and Gauleiter in Franconia Julius Streicher; and Commissioner for the Occupied Netherlands Arthur Seyss-Inquart. Their ashes were strewn in an estuary of the Isar river. Hermann Göring was also sentenced to death but committed suicide before he could be executed. The Nazi Party organizer Martin Borman was sentence to death in absentia.

LESSER SENTENCES

The Nazi economist Walter Funk and Erich Raeder, commander-in-chief of the navy, were sentenced to life imprisonment but were released in the 1950s due to illness. Rudolf Hess also got life imprisonment and committed suicide in Spandau prison in 1987. Hitler's successor Admiral Karl

Nuremburg trials (LEFT)
The trial of Josef Kramer, Commandant of Bergen-Belsen, 1945.

Nazis on trial (ABOVE)
Leading Nazis Hermann Goering and Rudolf Hess at Nuremberg, on trial for war crimes, 1946.

Dönitz received 10 years imprisonment, and Munitions Minister Albert Speer 20. Baldur von Schirach, gauleiter of Vienna, also got 20 years in prison. Konstantin von Neurath, protector of Bohemia and Moravia, got 15 years in prison. Three defendants were acquitted, but were imprisoned on other charges. Guilty verdicts were also handed down on the NSDAP, the SS, the SD, and the Gestapo. A US tribunal also sat at Nuremberg and, on December 9, 1946, proceedings began against 23 German doctors responsible for the Nazi "euthanasia" program to murder the mentally retarded and for medical experiments on concentration-camp inmates. Sixteen were found guilty; seven executed. In subsequent proceedings, 10,000 Germans were convicted and 250 sentenced to death.

TOKYO TRIALS

The Potsdam Declaration called for the trial of those who had "deceived and misled" the Japanese people into war. As commander of the occupation, General MacArthur arrested 39 suspects, mostly members of General Tojo's war cabinet. Tojo himself tried to commit suicide but was resuscitated by American doctors. MacArthur had already held war-crimes trials in Manila, resulting in the executions of Generals Yamashita and Homma. The Tokyo trials began on May 3, 1946, and on November 4, 1948, all the defendants were found guilty. Seven were sentenced to death, 16 to life terms, and two to lesser terms. Two had died during the trials and one had been found insane. On December 23, 1948, General Tojo and six others were hanged at Sugamo prison. Asian countries that had suffered under the Japanese occupation tried an estimated 5,000 suspected war criminals, executing some 900 and sentencing more than half to life in prison.

The cost of the war

"I know not with what weapons World War III will be fought,

but World War IV will be fought with sticks and stones."

Albert Einstein

There can be no accurate accounting for World War II. Only the casualty figures provided by the US and the British Commonwealth can be accepted as in any way accurate. In the Soviet Union and China the dead often went uncounted. For the Axis powers, where whole armies were destroyed and dispersed, and entire cities obliterated, losses can only be guessed at.

Estimates of the number of people who lost their lives during World War II vary from 35 million to 60 million, though the commonly accepted figure is 55 million. Few attempts have been made to estimate how many were wounded or permanently disabled. The best estimate for the Russian losses, including civilians, is 18 million dead; Germany 4,280,000 dead and five million military wounded. China is thought to have lost 1,310,000 men at arms and 1,752,951 wounded; the millions of civilians who died due to battle, bombardment, and murder, and who died of famine and pestilence caused by the war, were not counted. Japan lost 1,300,000 servicemen, four million were wounded and 672,000 civilians died. Poland lost 5,675,000 and some 5.7 million Jews were murdered in the death camps. The US got off comparatively lightly with 298,131 dead, including 6,000 civilians, and 671,801 wounded. Britain lost 357,116 dead, including 92,673 civilians, and 277,077 military wounded, while the British Commonwealth as a whole lost 466,045 dead and 475,047 wounded. Poland lost around 20 percent of its prewar population, Russia and Yugoslavia around 10 percent, and Germany only slightly less.

HOMELESSNESS

In Britain, around 2 million homes were destroyed. In Greece, France, Belgium, and The Netherlands, around 20 percent of all homes were destroyed. Poland also lost around 30 percent of its buildings, as well as 60 percent of its schools, scientific institutions and public buildings. The US Strategic Bombing Survey found that in Germany's 49 largest cities, 39 percent of the homes had been destroyed. Forty percent of the built-up areas of 66 Japanese cities were destroyed, and around 30 percent of Japan's urban population had lost their homes and possessions. In Europe there were an estimated 21 million refugees, more than half of them people who had been deported from their homelands as forced labor. The roads were further clogged by five million Soviet prisoners of war and forced laborers making their way home, while over eight million Germans fled westwards to escape the Soviet zone of occupation. China lost most of its hospitals and suffered floods and epidemics, while India suffered a famine which was not helped by the strain that the military authorities put on the economy.

ONE TRILLION DOLLARS

It is estimated that governments spent over one trillion dollars prosecuting the war. But that does not take into account the damage caused to the economy by the slaughter of able-bodied men, the destruction of factories, shops and the infrastructure, or the contribution of forced labor. Nor is it possible to put a monetary value on the misery, suffering and deprivation caused by the war.

POSTWAR RECONSTRUCTION

Europe, Japan, and much of the Far East were in a state of devastation after World War II. Of the participants, only the United States came through the fighting with its homeland unscathed. So it fell to the US to make good the damage, if only to prevent the nations wrecked by the war—both friend and former foe—falling to Communism.

The United Nations Relief and Rehabilitation Administration was created at a conference of 44 at the White House on November 9, 1943. Its aim was to provide economic assistance to Europe after the war and to look after and repatriate refugees. The US government provided nearly half of the funding for the UNRRA, which administered hundreds of camps for displaced persons in Germany, Italy, and Austria. It provided health and welfare assistance, as well as vocational training and entertainment, and helped repatriate millions of refugees. In 1947 the International Refugee Organization took over. It still had 643,000 displaced persons in its care in 1948.

MARSHALL PLAN

In 1947 US Secretary of State George C. Marshall feared that the poverty, dislocation, and unemployment caused by the war were boosting support for the Communist Party in Western Europe. On April 3, 1948, President Truman signed the European Recovery Program which distributed 13 billion dollars over the next four years to Austria, Belgium, Denmark, France, Greece, Iceland, Ireland, Italy, Luxembourg, The Netherlands, Norway, Portugal, Sweden, Switzerland, Turkey, the United Kingdom, and West Germany. The aim was to improve financial stability, restore agricultural and industrial production, and promote trade. The Marshall Plan proved a great success. The countries involved recorded a rise in gross national product of between 15 and 25 percent over the period. In 1949, it was extended to underdeveloped countries around the world.

COMECON

The Marshall Plan was offered to the Eastern European nations under Soviet military occupation in 1947. But, early on, the Soviet Union withdrew from the plan, followed by its satellite countries. Moscow then set up its equivalent, the Council for Mutual Economic Assistance—Comecon. The original members were Bulgaria, Czechoslovakia, Hungary, Poland, Romania, and the Soviet Union itself. Later, Albania, Cuba, East Germany, Mongolia, and Vietnam joined.

THE AIM OF THE MARSHALL PLAN

"Our policy is directed not against any country or doctrine but against hunger, poverty, desperation, and chaos. Its purpose should be the revival of a working economy in the world so as to permit the emergence of political and social conditions in which free institutions can exist."

George C. Marshall, Harvard University, June 5, 1947.

The ultimate price
The US Army cemetery at Omaha beach, Normandy, France.

Index

Picture Credits

Alamy: 1, 190. Getty Images: Sean Gallup, 189; Hugo Jaeger 4. Getty Images/AFP: 152. Getty Images/Anthony Potter Collection: 29. Getty Images/British Official Photo: 134. Getty Images/Fox Photos: 2, 22, 37, 46, 58tl, 66bl, 179; Reg Speller 106. Getty Images/Hulton Archive: 9, 11tl, 14, 29, 30bl, 31, 32b; 35, 43br, 85, 110, 145tl, 146, 219; R. Gates 147r; Herbert Gehr 207; Keystone: 6, 10, 17t, 20r, 44, 48, 50, 52, 55, 56, 60bl, 61, 63, 65, 70, 72, 92, 94, 103, 105, 119r, 120, 125, 127, 129, 132, 141, 148, 150, 164, 167, 171, 181, 186, 190, 197, 211; Fred Ramage 193, 202; V. Tomin 217 (main); William Vanderson 39b; Georgi Zemla 118. Getty Images/MPI: 75, 163.Getty Images/Picture Post: 184, 138. Getty Images/Popperfoto: 19, 24, 42, 81, 83, 90, 98, 101, 108, 126, 142, 158, 161. Getty Images/Three Lions: 29tl, 209. Getty Images/Time & Life Pictures: 67tl, 73tr, 76, 86, 96, 152, 183, 207, 215; Eliot Elisofon 112, 115br, 122b; Heinrich Hoffman: 207b; James Jarche: 68b; Louis R. Lowery: 194; Thomas D. McAvoy: 198; Leonard McCombe 221b; Mydans, Carl 173; Frank Scherschell, 155cl; Eugene W. Smith 136, US Marine Corps 117b; US Army 168, 175br, 176, 211. Getty Images/Topical Press Archive: 26, 37t. Jupiter Image: 19t. Mirrorpix: 7br, 9tl, 13, tr, 16, bl, tr, br, 27tl, 37r, 39t, 40t, 53t, 56r, 57br, 59, 63tr, tl, bl 78, 79tr, 89br, 101t, 121t, 123tl, 134br, 139tl, 145, 154, 157, 178br, 181tr, 188bl, 201tr, 203tr, tl, 207t, 212bl, 218.

With special thanks to the Department of History, United States Military Academy and the US National Archives and Records Administration.

Every effort has been made to obtain permission to reproduce copyright material, but there may be cases where we have been unable to trace a copyright holder. The publisher will be happy to correct any omissions in the future printings.